Where There's a Will . . .

Where There's a Will...

Who Inherited What and Why

Stephen M. Silverman

HarperCollins*Publishers*

FIRST EDITION

Designed by Cassandra J. Pappas

Library of Congress Cataloging-in-Publication Data

Silverman, Stephen M.
    Where there's a will—Stephen M. Silverman.
        p.   cm.
    Includes index.
    ISBN 0-06-016260-0
    1. Celebrities—United States—Biography. 2. Wills—United
States. 3. Biography—20th century.   I. Title.
CT220.S55   1991
920.073—dc20   89-46557

91 92 93 94 95 CC/RRD 10 9 8 7 6 5 4 3 2 1

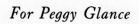

For Peggy Glance

Contents

Contents ix

Acknowledgments

For invaluable assistance and godlike patience, the author wishes to bequeath his thanks everlasting to the following:

Lawrence P. Ashmead, Carol Atkinson, Marci Burstiner, Miles P. Finley, Renee Furst, Alfred P. Lowman, John Michel, Heidi Siegmund, Cathy Stephens, and Pauline Sweezey, chief economist for the State of California.

Introduction

JOHN F. KENNEDY LEFT NO WILL. LIKE THE
rest of us, he did not expect his life would end in 1963. Come-
dian Lenny Bruce, dead at age forty in 1966, also did not leave
a will. Looking back sympathetically at his final ten years, it
seems obvious that someone should have advised Bruce to get
his affairs in order.

Marilyn Monroe is another story. Constantly surrounded
by attorneys, managers, and agents, she regularly revised her
will. Her final testament, dated January 14, 1961, was signed
only one year and seven months before she died. As reported
in the papers of probate, her attorney "described MISS
MONROE as being 'in complete possession of her faculties,'
'astute,' and 'above normal in intelligence.' In discussing business with her he found her to 'understand the nature and
import of the various matters.' On the execution of the Will,
she 'understood the nature of her act,' did not 'appear to be

under duress at any time,' and was not 'emotionally disturbed.' An analysis of the Will in the light of MARILYN MONROE'S background establishes what appears to be a rational, orderly disposition of her estate."

If only there had been a rational, orderly disposition of her life—but, then, who can alter the inevitable?

This book was inspired by the simple query of a friend as to why Cary Grant, who left an estate valued at $50 million, chose to remember a specific British journalist with $25,000. (The reason was simply friendship, not because of blackmail, as fantasized.) So, this book is an attempt to probe the lives and deaths of various celebrated people by tapping into their voices from the grave—their last wills and testaments.

Gruesome? Certainly not. Uplifting? Sometimes. Sad? Frequently. Despite often specific intentions, in most cases— after jilted relatives and most especially lawyers and the tax people finish with an estate—the deceased seldom fully gets his or her way.

In a few rare cases, though, pleasant surprises can develop. Orson Welles's will (he died in 1985) left his Las Vegas house and most of his remaining estate to a Yugoslavian actress, Oja Kodar (née Olka Palinkas), because he fell in love with her. Far more beneficial to the rest of us was a small proviso in Welles's will prohibiting any tampering with his works. As a result, American telecommunications baron Ted Turner was stopped dead in court from colorizing Welles's 1941 classic *Citizen Kane*. Thank you, Orson.

Another happy incident: In an 80–20 split, Valerie Eliot, widow of poet T. S. Eliot (d. 1965), and Eliot's British publisher Faber and Faber were both enjoying a pleasant income, nothing more, from the collected poems and plays of the literary giant. Then, in 1981, composer Andrew Lloyd Webber set to music one of Eliot's lesser works, *Old Possum's Book of Practical Cats,* called it *Cats,* and Mrs. Eliot and Faber and Faber are now sharing about $3.5 million per annum from that book alone.

But then there are the fights. In the course of researching this book in the Surrogate's Courts of New York and Los Angeles, I was alerted to expect a call from the granddaughter of an actor who was best known for his gangster roles. The actor had died in 1973, and here, seventeen years later, his relatives were still squabbling. My request to see the file sent up a red flag; I was to be interrogated to insure I was not an attorney for one of the opposing sides.

The fights are usually nothing less than bitter, even when no will exists. In the case of Lenny Bruce, his mother Sally Marr and daughter Kitty Bruce at one point were pitted against one another to see who owned Lenny's right to his likeness. The dispute arose because of a feature-movie depiction of Bruce's life, *Lenny.* In California, both Bruces are now protected thanks to legislation passed in 1985, giving the legal heirs of deceased celebrities the right to the dearly departed's name and likeness. (The biggest breadwinner in that sweepstakes over the past few years has been Marilyn Monroe.)

Generally, wills are signed in the offices of attorneys, but there are exceptions. Adolf Hitler signed his in his Berlin bunker one day before he allegedly took his own life. Der Fuehrer willed his remaining worldly possessions to the party, "or, if this no longer exists, to the state." Ernest Hemingway wrote his will in Cuba, and, true to his style, kept it short.

My favorite anecdote associated with the signing of a will involves the choreographer Bob Fosse and his pal, the playwright Paddy Chayefsky. On the eve of Fosse's undergoing an operation for open heart surgery, his lawyers prepared his will, and Chayefsky paid Fosse a bedside visit in New York Hospital. Fosse requested that his friend read and sign the document.

"Am I in it?" asked Chayefsky.

"No," Fosse informed him, "you're the witness."

"Then fuck you," replied Chayefsky. "Live!"

While most wills reflect a writing style that is dry and filled with legalese, here, too, some exceptions exist. F. Scott Fitzgerald's document dated June 17, 1937, reveals a great deal about the writer, who amended his requests in his own hand only six weeks before he died on December 21, 1940. Item one stated, "I will and direct that at my death my executors . . . provide for me a suitable funeral and burial in keeping with my station in life." With his pen Fitzgerald, who since the mid-1930s had felt his life was on the skids, crossed out "a suitable" as the description of his desired funeral and substituted above it, "the cheapest." Then he struck a line through the phrase "in keeping with my station in life."

Noted misanthrope—and closet bigot—William Claude Fields (1879–1946) likewise injected his personality into his last testament. In the document dated April 28, 1943, Fields ordered that after the death of his principal beneficiaries—his brother, sister, and last girl friend—"I direct that my executors procure the organization of a membership or other approved corporation under the name W. C. FIELDS COLLEGE for orphan white boys and girls, where no religion of any sort is to be preached. Harmony is the purpose of this thought. It is my desire the college will be built in California in Los Angeles."

It didn't happen. Fields's estranged wife attached herself to the will and the targeted charity money was never to be garnered. (A real Fields touch: His wife must have truly despised him; in the probate papers, it is stated that, "Under the will the decedent had directed that his body be cremated. The widow, through her counsel, instructed the Forest Lawn [cemetery] to have him buried.")

If there appears to be a preponderance of show business names in this book, this is no accident. High-profile lives frequently result in high-profile deaths. In addition, through technology show business personalities have the capacity to keep generating income long after their physical bodies and talents leave this earth. Even before the advent of home video, this could be the case. Once again, let's look at Marilyn Monroe. In the year immediately following her death, her estate was expecting to receive 10 percent of the distributor's gross from two of her films, *Some Like It Hot* and *The Misfits*. Monroe's share was calculated to be $510,930.61 from the first film, and $86,820.01 from the latter—"subject to United States income tax withholding, State income tax withholding, agent's commission, Motion Picture Relief Fund deductions, and other nominal payroll taxes." (Sadly, Monroe was in hock at the time of her demise, so a lot of that expected income would not have been hers even if she had lived.)

There are perhaps lessons to be gained from what follows here. However, the purpose in gathering this information was not to be didactic, but rather to satisfy some morbid and some equally healthy curiosity and, in some way, set about measuring a few interesting lives and how they were led.

Truth to tell, there is a revelation that surfaced, not so much in the researching of this book, but in its writing. In its typing, actually.

And that is, the difference between owning and owing. It's only one letter.

STEPHEN M. SILVERMAN
New York City
August 1990

John Jacob Astor

WHEN SOMEONE HAS THE KIND OF MONEY old man Astor was sitting on when he died, he can pretty much reach into the future and write it. Which is exactly what Astor did. Having owned so much of what is now New York City, he wrote a will that reads a bit like an international treaty partitioning Western Europe after World War I.

Astor died $20 million to the good in 1848. That's approximately $103 million in 1990 dollars, a pittance compared to some of today's multibillionaires, but it was the largest fortune in the New World at the time, and that alone earned him a Trump-like notoriety.

In retrospect, what makes Astor's estate even more fantastic is that basically he amassed it from nothing, and even nearly went broke several times in the process. Astor was born in Walldorf, Germany, on July 17, 1763, the son of a butcher. After spending a couple of years in London working with his brother in a musical instrument store, Astor arrived in New York in 1783, at the end of the Revolution, and continued in the business. His real passion, however, turned out to be the fur trade, in upper New York State and Canada, where he tramped through wilderness territory that up until then had been the exclusive domain of the Indians. A heavy load of pelts strapped to his back, and over his shoulder a musket, his face dirty and bitten by black flies, Astor roamed those woods for seventeen years, eventually parlaying that sweaty equity—plus a few loans—into a small fortune estimated at $250,000.

Astor's fur trade grew by hook and possibly by crook—today he might have wound up in jail for insider trading or fraud—until it reached around the globe. His fleet operated in the Baltic and Mediterranean and around the Pacific Rim, trading in pelts and commodities that could be swapped for furs. In his first shipment to Canton—trading furs for ginseng, which in China he exchanged for tea, which in New York he sold for cash—he made a profit of $55,000.

But the real money came from real estate. Astor bought up farms on Manhattan, which in those days was mostly rural and thinly settled. His was a talent for sniffing out distressed parcels of land and then offering the owner a pittance to take over the mortgage; or he'd acquire the mortgage of some landowner who was struggling to make ends meet, and then squeeze him out of the deed. By all accounts he was shrewd, ruthless, and a skinflint.

His timing could not have been more perfect. New York subsequently went through a boom that provided Astor with his real fortune, usually without his ever selling the land. It was Astor who established the practice of giving long-term leases to build on his real estate holdings.

By the time he died, Astor was the richest and most detested landlord in New York. He owned the largest hotel in the world, but also vast slums in which humans lived in more wretched conditions than the horses in his private stables. Astor owned so much of the city, and had made so much money from it, that a populist newspaper columnist at the time of the mogul's death wrote that half of the Astor wealth "belongs to the people of the city of New York. . . . It is plain as that two and two make four, that . . . half of his immense estate, in its actual value, has accrued to him [from] the industry of the community."

Astor, who once said, "The disposition to do good does not always increase with the means," left half of his $20 million estate to his second son, William, and the other half in trust so William could retain the vast family real estate holdings. Astor's major philanthropic bequest was the $400,000 he left—"desiring to render a public benefit to the City of New York and to contribute to the advancement of useful knowledge and the general good of society"—to establish a public library in New York. The library was to be built on land he owned on Lafayette Street, in the part of New York that is known today as the East Village. But merged in later years with other gifts from wealthy New Yorkers, the funds established the main branch of the New York Public Library uptown, at Fifth Avenue and Forty-second Street. Astor's words, "The Advancement of Useful Knowledge," are etched in stone over the front entrance.

Much of the remainder of his generosity benefited immigrants such as himself through the German Society of New York. It was to receive $30,000 (later reduced to $20,000, because of gifts he had made to it during his lifetime) "to buy and maintain an office and to hire German-speaking attendants for the purpose of giving free advice and information for all emigrants arriving in New York." In his original will he left $25,000 for Columbia College "to establish a professorship of the German language and literature," but it was later revoked. He also left $25,000 to the Association for the Relief of Respectable Aged and Indigent Females, also reduced before he died. He did kick in something for the folks back home: $50,000 for "the use of the poor of Walldorf near Heidelberg in the Grand Duchy of Baden by the establishment of some provision for the sick or disabled or the education and improvement of the young who may be in a condition to need the aid of such fund."

Because his wife and one of his daughters predeceased him, and because his first son was insane, Astor named his second son, William, as his principal heir. But the will provides a long list of lump sums, annuities, and parcels of land for various individuals that add up to a kind of dividing-up-of-the-spoils from his looting of New York City.

To his daughter, Dorothea, he left use of all the household furniture for life as well as all the silver plate "except the new service of plate." Also, the income from $100,000 in New York City bonds; 500 shares of capital stock in the Bank of America; 1,000 shares of capital stock in the Manhattan Company; $25,000 deposited with the New York Life Insurance and Trust Company; "all of which income I devote expressly to her sole and separate use to be at her own disposal when received by her and . . . otherwise to be free from all claims, interest, or interference of her husband."

He also left her a house and lot on Lafayette Place "being

27'6" wide and 137'6" deep to hold the same during her natural life."

He left to Dorothea's children "all my lots on the easterly side of Lafayette Place and fronting thereon also my lots in the rear of my lots on said easterly side extending to the Bowery. Also my lands between Charleston Street, Morton Street, Greenwich Street, and the Hudson River." This amounted to more than 100 parcels of land.

To his favorite grandson, Charles Bristed, Astor left property all over the city, extending from lower Broadway to what is today midtown in the garment district along Seventh Avenue.

Astor directed that his executors "provide for my unfortunate [insane] son John Jacob and to procure for him all the comforts which his condition doth or may admit and to bear the expense thereof not exceeding $5,000 a year [later raised to $10,000 by a codicil]. And in case he should be restored [to sanity] then I direct them to apply to his use $100,000 a year during his life." J.J. was not restored to sanity. Astor also provided him with a house on Fourteenth Street.

William, fortunately, proved not only perfectly sane but an astute businessman. Stingy like his father, he built up an even larger fortune out of tenement housing as the flow of immigration grew into a deluge. He left an estate valued at almost $50 million when he died in 1875. One of his sons, in turn, left an estate of $75 million, and the other, John Jacob IV, left $87 million when he went down on H. M. S. *Titanic* in 1912.

William Vincent Astor, John Jacob's great-grandson, died childless in 1959 after three marriages. His estate was worth $120 million, or about $480 million in 1990 dollars. Vincent rejected the slum legacy of the family and allied himself with the New Deal politics of Franklin D. Roosevelt. The little people finally got back some of that Astor loot, in the half of his fortune that he left to the Vincent Astor Foundation, "to alleviate human misery" mainly through medical research. The other half went to his widow, the former Brooke Russell Marshall.

W. H. Auden

When it comes, will it come without warning
    Just as I'm picking my nose,
Will it knock on my door in the morning
    Or tread in the bus on my toes,
Will it come like a change in the weather,
    Will its greeting be courteous or bluff,
Will it alter my life altogether?
    O tell me the truth about love.

                      —W. H. Auden

WYSTAN HUGH AUDEN IS REMEMBERED BY his admirers as an undisputed master of English poetry, one who examined and expressed the human condition through verse that was vibrant, painfully on the mark, and often dealt with contemporary issues including the eternities of love and mortality. As one critic expressed it, no other poet "has shown such an extraordinary capacity to speak through poetry, with a poet's vision, about the whole of life."

Still, it was love that seemed to fuel Auden's creative engine through most of his life, and it was love that defined his last will and testament.

Born on February 21, 1907, Auden came into his art

early, at Christ Church College in Oxford, England, in the 1920s. His father was a professor of public health and his mother was a nurse. He grew up in Birmingham, England, and originally set out on a career in science.

In no time, however, he fell in with a group of other budding writers in college, including Christopher Isherwood and Stephen Spender, and soon regarded himself, not completely unjustifiably, as the leader of a new movement in English literature. Spender would later say that "a group of emergent artists existed in his mind, like a cabinet in the mind of a party leader." Many of them, like Auden, were homosexual and in addition to their art they shared the intimate details of their romantic lives with each other, organizing a kind of underground society of gay writers.

Like others in his social circle, Auden gave heterosexuality a chance, although his forays amounted to little. He shared a couple of limp affairs with women, and even asked one to marry him once when he was on the rebound from an afflicted male affair. He did marry; the union was set up by Isherwood to save Erika Mann, daughter of the German author Thomas Mann, from the Nazis just before World War II by giving her a second citizenship. She was a lesbian.

Auden was very popular in England, although his success was mainly critical, so that he was nearly out of money in 1939 when he arrived with Isherwood to live and write in New York. Disenchanted with England and with Europe, where Auden had done extensive traveling and literary collaborating with Isherwood, they had decided to give the States a try, initially to write a guidebook about America.

Within a few months of arriving in the metropolis, Auden met the young man who would alter as well as define the remaining thirty-four years of his life, and become his only true heir. Auden met Chester Simon Kallman on April 6, 1939. Kallman, then an eighteen-year-old Brooklyn College student, attended a reading in New York by Auden and Isherwood, where he and a friend sat in the front row and flirted with Auden and Isherwood.

The two young men then went on stage when the reading finished and asked if they could interview Auden for their college magazine. Auden was vague, but Isherwood gave them the address of the apartment he and Auden shared on Manhattan's East 81st Street. Kallman showed up two days later, alone. Auden was at first irritated, having expected a different young man he'd had his eye on at the reading. He muttered something to Isherwood about the visitor being "the wrong blond."

Yet something clicked between them, and in jig time a romance was ablaze. Kallman, who was fourteen years younger than Auden, was the oldest son of a Manhattan dentist. His mother had died when he was four, and he'd had two stepmothers who he later claimed treated him badly. As a youth Kallman was described as looking both angelic and demonic; in any event, Auden fancied him a great deal. A few weeks after their meeting, Auden wrote to a friend, "I know that Love as a fever does not last, but for some years now I've known that the one thing I really needed was marriage, and I think I have enough experience and judgment to know that this relationship is going to be marriage with all its boredoms and rewards."

Within weeks Kallman had become the center of Auden's life. "You are to me, emotionally a mother, physically a father, and intellectually a son . . . I believe in your creative gift . . . I rely absolutely upon your critical judgment . . . With my body, I worship yours," Auden would later write to Kallman, although within a couple of years their relationship became less physical. Kallman set out upon many affairs, and Auden occasionally went crazy with jealousy, later confessing to Kallman, "On account of you I have been in intention and almost in act, a murderer."

They lived together only intermittently, yet they often traveled in tandem, and in fact collaborated on several projects including two operas, one for Stravinsky, called *The Rake's Progress,* and another, *Love's Labour's Lost.*

Auden and Kallman both lived the hard-drinking lifestyle of writers in their generations. For some twenty years Auden was addicted to Benzedrine to get him up in the morning and Seconal to put him to sleep at night. In between he drank profusely until, near the end of his life, when he found the pills harder to procure, he took to keeping a glass of vodka by his bed in case he woke up in the middle of the night and needed something to knock him out until morning.

Eventually Auden took out U.S. citizenship and became a permanent resident of New York. Kallman increasingly spent time in distant places, finally settling for long stretches in Greece, while his money went toward pursuing sex with anyone who would have him. Becoming something of a derelict, he squandered whatever funds he collected for himself, and let Auden support him right up until the end.

Auden signed his last will in 1964, apparently in London, where the two witnesses to his signature lived. He left everything to Kallman or, in the event Kallman died first, to his two nieces, the daughters of his only brother.

His executors were to be the poet William Meredith and the literary critic Monroe Spears, both old friends. But in 1972 Auden developed second thoughts and approached Edward Mendelson, a young man in his mid-twenties who was on the faculty at the Yale University English department. Mendelson had written a doctoral thesis on Auden's poetry and was finishing a bibliography of Auden's complete works.

Mendelson collaborated with Auden on a retrospective collection of his book reviews and essays. Auden was never bold or self-assured about his sexuality, and he had recently undergone a kind of religious conversion. Because his letters were often full of specific details of his sex life, or lack thereof, Auden asked Mendelson to be his literary executor and ordered that, on his death, Mendelson should put notices in the U.S. and British press "requesting any friends who have letters from me to burn them when they're done with them and on no account to show them to anyone else." However, when Auden mentioned this request to several of his friends they informed him they would unequivocally ignore it.

As he grew older Auden worried about dying of a heart attack and not being discovered for days. He was living in a disheveled apartment on St. Mark's Place in New York's East Village at a time when the neighborhood was rundown and not on the regular route of any of his friends. He began to lobby for Christ Church College, in Oxford, to provide him with a secure and final place to live, as King's College, Cambridge, had done for E. M. Forster, another notable homosexual English writer near the end of his life. While Auden waited the two years it took for this request to be granted, he let himself go. He wore the same suit for months until it was covered with grease spots and worn out. Refusing to see doctors, he allowed his physical health to deteriorate.

A cottage was finally made available at Christ Church in 1972. Auden, packing to move to Oxford, picked a few books out of his library to take with him, and contacted a bookseller to dispose of the rest, after inviting friends to help themselves, saying, "Take a book, some books, anything you want."

The end came a little more than a year later. It was not in Oxford but near Vienna, in a tiny town named Kirchstetten, where Auden had bought a house and had spent untold blocks of time over the years cohabiting and collaborating with Kallman. At the time, Kallman was traveling with Auden, and was the person who discovered his dead body in the hotel room where Auden had gone to sleep shortly after giving a poetry reading.

Auden died the night of September 28, 1973 of a heart attack and complications of alcoholism. The funeral was held in Kirchstetten, where he'd wanted to be buried. The ending, after all, was tidy.

The will was short, four pages, not including the signature page, and included his directive that "My executors . . . destroy all personal correspondence that shall be in my possession at the time of my death and further . . . that they shall make public in the most effective manner, my wish that all persons who may be in possession of letters written by me, whatever their content, shall destroy the same."

Auden left an estate valued at about $250,000 (approximately $875,000 in 1990 dollars), meager considering his stature in the literary world. Any possible claim by his legal wife, Erika Mann, was obviated by her death in 1969. There were no children.

A handwritten accounting of his assets at the time of death, attached to an estate tax return, lists manuscripts worth $28,500 and royalties due of $80,000. Presumably his estate included the Austrian house, but Kallman, who in addition to being an alcoholic, also mistrusted lawyers, made a mess of what was left. He sold the house without legal papers to Auden's housekeeper for a lifetime annuity of $125 a month and then traipsed off to assuage his grief by squandering what small income Auden had bequeathed him.

Kallman was literally wrecked by Auden's death. What little remained of him after those years of debauchery now began to fall to pieces. He finally died in Athens in 1975 at the age of fifty-four, apparently of heart failure, two years after Auden.

Kallman's will left everything except personal belongings to Auden. That meant Kallman's father, the dentist who by then was well into his eighties, automatically became his heir. But Kallman had already given all of Auden's papers to Mendelson, the literary executor, and told Mendelson to donate them to the New York Public Library. Kallman's father sued for return of the papers, but in the end he managed to retain only the copyrights and royalties. The papers themselves remained in the library.

Near the close of a long, celebrated, illustrious career that included the Pulitzer Prize for poetry in 1948, the King's Gold Medal for poetry, and a host of other prizes and honors for his verse, Auden wrote, "In the end, art is small beer. The really serious things in life are earning one's living so as not to be a parasite, and loving one's neighbour." A romantic to the end.

P. T. Barnum

IT MAY BE TRUE, AS THE SAYING GOES, THAT there's a sucker born every minute. But the scholars are pretty much unanimous that the first person to articulate the observation was not Phineas Taylor Barnum, as popular history would have us believe. That is not to say that Barnum would have disagreed with the statement. This con man extraordinaire made a fortune fooling the masses into swallowing, and paying to see, some of the world's most unbelievable hoaxes. He once, in 1835, made a deal with another huckster to buy the right to exhibit a very wrinkled, very old slave woman who he then claimed was 161 years old and had been George Washington's nurse. Fortunately or unfortunately for Barnum, the poor woman died soon after he put her on display in his Bridgeport, Connecticut, museum—before anyone came around to dispute or authenticate her age.

Barnum was—and with a bit of luck will always remain—the boldest, most innovative, most successful, and most tasteless show business promoter who ever lived. He was among the first to define the limits of popular American trash culture, and make his fortune turning freaks of nature into media superstars. Taking a child with abnormal depigmentation (large white spots on black skin), Barnum nicknamed him the "Leopard Boy," threw him into a toga, and shoved him on display. He "created" the person of Tom Thumb for an infantine midget whom he dressed as Napoleon, added seven years to his age to make him seem even tinier, and sent him off on international tour.

Barnum died a rich old man of seventy-nine, with an estate valued at $4.3 million, a staggering sum in 1891. Most of this wealth was attributable to his half-ownership of Barnum and Bailey's "Greatest Show on Earth," a combination zoo, circus, theater, concert hall, museum, and freak show that literally offered something for everyone. His business partner during the last decade of his life, James Bailey, owned 25 percent. A third, forgotten individual, whose name never appeared on posters, owned the remaining quarter.

Barnum's will, written in excruciating detail, included eight codicils containing dozens of articles tacked onto it in the last year of his life. These long, torturous instructions, full of intricate directions and mathematical calculations, seemed to provide, like his show, something for everyone.

For instance, the estate would pay the rent for his wife, Nancy, in a house anywhere in the United States so long as she lived in it at least eighteen months every three years, with the rent not to exceed $1,000 a year. Or, instead, she could have a "life estate" on any vacant lot in Barnum's holdings except the house grounds of the mansion, and not more than thirty-six rods of land or land worth more than $3,000. The estate would build her a house, but it was not to cost more than $8,000, and then she had to live in it at least nine months every three years and pay the taxes and assessments herself.

Barnum went so far as to direct the disposition of his library, book by book, to various individuals. He disposed of his personal belongings piece by piece: to his daughter, Helen, "the gold watch worn by her mother and the ivory Madonna, also the two old tapestry pictures in the parlor and one gilt vase with gold set in Paris."

Among other quirks, Barnum was obsessed with how history would treat him. While still alive he instructed his staff to create scrapbooks of his press notices for his descendants, and donated clothing to Madame Tussaud's in London so his effigy could be properly attired. He made a wax cylinder recording in 1889, two years before he died, in which he expressed the hope that "my voice, like my great show, will reach future generations and be heard centuries after I have joined the great and, as I believe, happy majority."

Barnum orchestrated his death with the same meticulous attention to detail and publicity that made his circus successful. He was still giving press interviews almost up to the day he died from atherosclerosis, or heart failure resulting from "fatty degeneration of the heart." The last interview he gave appeared in the *Newtown* (Connecticut) *Bee* on the day he was buried, April 10, 1891. Barnum openly, if weakly, had discussed with the reporter the arrangements for his imminent funeral. It would, he explained, be in the "English custom," with the remains viewed only by close relatives, rather than letting the great unwashed file by the bier, gawking and commenting on his appearance like the freaks in his shows. The "Prince of Humbug," as he had come to be known, was going to go out in royal style.

His body, preserved on ice, lay in a dark room at his estate in Bridgeport for two days before the funeral. Following private services at the house, the casket was hauled to the city's largest house of worship, South Congregational, where the pastor conducted a public ceremony. The route from the mansion to the church and then to the cemetery was packed with crowds. Businesses shut down and buildings were draped with crepe. The circus, which was performing at New York's Madison Square Garden at the time, canceled performances out of respect.

In his original will, dated January 30, 1888, Barnum left his second wife Nancy (his first wife Charity had died) the grand sum of $500, but added a provision that she receive an annuity of $2,500 a year for the rest of her life, in accordance with a contract they had signed when they married. Then he added an additional yearly $6,500 from his estate. He left each of his four daughters, who were products of his first marriage, $5,000.

In time he grew more generous, and by his death the will had been altered so that Nancy Barnum was to receive $40,000 a year as long as she lived plus a cash payment of $100,000. His daughters were also presented with more money, some of it reduced by loans they had received while the patriarch was still alive.

Barnum's will was as complicated as a leveraged buyout. It specified that his wife should inherit "all the articles of moveable furniture including all the bedding, bed and table linen, carpets, curtains, plates, porcelain, books, statuary, pictures, house decorations, and ornaments," "the best piano of which I shall die possessed," "any and all horses, harnesses, saddles, carriages, and sleighs," "my diamond pin, chain and holder usually worn by me," "my stereoscope box or instrument with all stereoscopic slides or pictures and all photographs and albums except my family album," "life use of my garden or lawn statuary fountain and all house lawn or garden utensils or implements."

He left an assortment of personal objects to his daughters and grandchildren: "my old family Bible," "two old tapestry pictures in the parlor," "the oil painting scene in the Adirondacks, now in my bedroom." The details went on for pages.

Because, long before Barnum died, it was clear that he was going to leave no legitimate male heirs (he did produce a bastard son who became a doctor), let alone any offspring interested in running his business enterprises, the showman made an unusual deal with his oldest grandson that is described in the will:

"Whereas I have no son, and therefore my name of Barnum will not otherwise be continued in my family except by my wife and as I would like to perpetuate my surname and I have deep love and respect for, and confidence in the strict integrity of my said grandson Clinton H. Seeley who I am sure will honor the name, therefore I give to my grandson Clinton H. Seeley $25,000 on this express condition that he shall in a legal and proper way change his name or cause his name to be changed to that of Clinton Barnum Seeley and that he shall habitually use the name of Barnum either as Clinton Barnum Seeley or C. Barnum Seeley or Barnum Seeley in his name so that the name of Barnum shall always be known as his name."

Clinton, being no sucker himself, did change his name. Among other enticements, Barnum had set Clinton up in the stock market with an income of $2,000. But then Barnum went on to try to coax Clinton into taking his place at the helm of Barnum and Bailey. He offered Clinton three percent of the net profits of Barnum's interest in the shows if he would "faithfully devote so much of his person and attention to the interests of such shows and of my estate in general and render such service for the same as shall satisfy my [executors] or a majority of them that he is entitled to it." Clinton's yearly income was to be at least $5,000 a year but not more than $10,000. When he traveled with the show, Clinton was to "receive as good accommodations as any of the partners and will be required to do no more menial work."

Clinton, as it happened, found this was an offer that he could refuse. He traveled with the show for a couple of seasons at most, but did not take to the life. The problem may have been that Clinton and Bailey did not get along.

After his death, according to *The New York Times,* Clinton spent most of his time in the city and on his yacht, *The Atlantic.* Bailey refused to hire Clinton, as the will provided for, so Clinton sued for his portion of the show's profits. It is not clear if any were ever received.

Upon Barnum's death, his executors wasted no time in liquidating his entertainment properties, although they had to wait to sell off his share of the big top. Barnum had stipulated that his estate should continue to own the "Greatest Show on Earth" for three years after his death, setting aside $200,000 for his share of the operating expenses, "to meet the outlays for the successful prosecution of said business in an honorable, respectable, and strictly moral manner with a view to refine and elevate such recreations and to edify and instruct as well as innocently amuse those who attend them."

In 1894, as soon as this provision expired, Bailey bought Barnum's half of the business. (After Bailey died in 1906, the Ringling Brothers acquired it and added their name to the letterhead.) With most of the non–real estate assets disposed of, the cash was quickly and unceremoniously divided between

Nancy Barnum and Barnum's daughters by his first wife and their children. Clinton and three members of his family were able to split $325,000. (The bulk of the estate was tied up in income-producing real estate which was held aside to keep paying Nancy Barnum's $40,000-a-year allowance.)

Generous he was. Although Barnum was perhaps history's greatest perpetrator of relatively innocent hoaxes and frauds, he was also remembered as a giving and religious man. He did not drink, believed in temperance for others, and gave large sums to charitable causes, particularly when it allowed him to slap his name on a building. He left $5,000 to a religious publishing company for the specific purpose of printing and distributing copies of a sermon titled "The Victory of Christ," and two pamphlets: *213 Questions Without Answers* and *Universalism, What It Is and What It's Good For.* The literature was to be distributed free or at cost.

Yet neither was Barnum a stick-in-the-mud. As a seasoned practical joker, he loved more than anything else to take advantage of another man's foolishness or stupidity and rub the victim's nose in it. One of those to whom he was particularly unmerciful was Henry Bergh, the first president of the American Society for the Prevention of Cruelty to Animals, based in New York. Bergh was a fanatic. His first act as president in 1866 was to go public with righteous indignation when he learned that Barnum's snake keepers at his New York "zoo" (which Barnum called the American Museum) were feeding live rabbits to the boa constrictors and charging people for the thrill of watching them being devoured.

Bergh tried to generate public support for his outrage, and even called for Barnum's arrest on cruelty charges. But Bergh wound up looking the dolt, thanks to the massive publicity machine that Barnum controlled by virtue of his huge reputation, to say nothing of the flood of advertising dollars Barnum regularly doled out to the local media. Boa constrictors won't eat dead meat, Barnum explained to his public; if they aren't fed live animals, they die. "In accordance with the laws of nature," he announced, the American Museum would continue to let the snakes feast on the cuddly little bunnies.

Bergh pressed on, suggesting that if Barnum were correct, then it was his obligation to let the boa constrictors die in order to save the rabbits. Barnum retaliated by publishing all of Bergh's previous hysterical letters to him on the subject, succeeding in the process in discrediting and ridiculing him.

But by the time he died some twenty-four years later, Barnum had reached some sort of understanding with Bergh, and the two men had found something to admire in each other. Barnum, Bergh had decided, was not an abuser of animals after all. In fact, he'd had a chance to watch the animal trainers up close and decided that Barnum could be considered a big supporter of the ASPCA.

Barnum, meanwhile, willed $1,000 to the city of Bridgeport to erect a statue of Bergh, "distinguished philanthropist and founder of the ASPCA."

John Belushi

ONE WOULD BE HARD PRESSED TO THINK OF John Belushi in any other context than that of the chaotic menagerie of characters he created for television's *Saturday Night Live*, as well as various film roles. His name alone quickly conjures up a list that includes a killer bee, a Samurai warrior, Bluto the *Animal House* mascot, and a Blues Brother. All of these frenetic creatures who came to define Belushi in the eyes of the public were, in a way, granitized by the seedy way in which he died, his body burned out on drugs, and the way he was buried, wearing engineer boots and Army pants with a motorcycle escort. A more hedonistic, alienated, counterculture example of his times one would be hard pressed to invent.

On the other hand, Belushi, who fatally overdosed on heroin and cocaine on March 5, 1982, at the age of thirty-three, left a twenty-two-page typewritten will that, by contrast, was as well-organized and precise as a good Swiss watch, and seemed to overflow with love and tenderness not only for his immediate family but also his in-laws. Although Belushi left everything to his wife and high school sweetheart, Judy Jacklin, his will contained the provision that if she had died first, his estate would be divided up evenly among eleven of his relatives, including Judy's parents, two sisters-in-law, and a brother-in-law. The language of the will is straightforward but doesn't give any hints as to why he was so generous, although Belushi had been supporting this enormous extended family for years through his corporate persona, Phantom Enterprises. The will, prepared in 1979, was obviously an extension of the largesse he was already doling out.

According to the reporter Bob Woodward in his 1984 book, *Wired,* Belushi's company was laying out nearly $4,400 a month in "salaries" for his father Adam ($625), his mother Agnes ($550), his sister Marian ($858), his younger brother Billy ($600), his father-in-law Robert Jacklin ($667), and his mother-in-law Jean Jacklin ($1,080). Phantom additionally paid out more than $4,000 a month in medical insurance premiums for family members on the payroll. By the time he died, Belushi was essentially supporting his parents. According to Woodward, he had also bailed his father out of $60,000 worth of debt connected with two failed Chicago restaurants. Woodward estimated that Belushi required an annual income of between $500,000 and $1 million simply to maintain this entourage as well as himself.

After Judy, the eleven family members who would have shared in the estate were his father and mother, his sister Marian, his brother Jim (also an actor), his brother Billy, his nephew Adam (Marian's son, who was eleven at the time Belushi died), his father-in-law Robert Jacklin, his mother-in-law Jean Jacklin, their son Rob, Judy's sister Pamela, and another sister-in-law, Patricia Brewster. Belushi's will contained a clause that cut out of the will anyone who tried to contest it. He named Mark Lipsky, his accountant, as executor.

The value of his estate is hard to pinpoint from court records, but in 1985 Judy listed it in an estate tax filing as almost $3.4 million. John owned a house near where he was buried on Martha's Vineyard; a Manhattan townhouse on West Tenth Street; a house in the old mining town of Julian, California (a tiny tourist village about sixty miles from San Diego); and a condominium in Addison, Illinois, near Chicago.

The house on Martha's Vineyard was appraised at $723,000 but carried a $300,000 mortgage. It had once been owned by Robert N. McNamara, the former Secretary of Defense, and included 450 feet of beach frontage that was once locally known as a nude beach, eight acres of land, and a large bedroom that Belushi had converted into a high-tech music and entertainment chamber filled with $15,000 worth of electronic and musical equipment. (According to the appraisal letter attached to the tax return, the doors had been removed from all the closets in the house and replaced with curtains. No reason was given.)

The townhouse was listed at $895,000, with a $500,000 mortgage outstanding. The California house was appraised at $210,000 and the Illinois condo's value at $60,000. The bulk of his spendable estate came from life insurance payoffs, more than $1 million.

Among the debts Belushi left behind when he died were: $139,673 payable to his longtime partner Dan Aykroyd's corporate entity, Black Rhino Enterprises; a $271 veterinary bill; $417 to MasterCard and $604 to VISA; $77 to a drugstore in

Julian; $112 to Illinois Bell (telephone company); and more than $4,000 to Budget Rent-A-Car.

The expenses of embalming his body, shipping it back East, feeding and housing the mourners, eulogizing and burying him came to almost $16,000.

With the money she inherited, Judy said she would establish a John Belushi Memorial Fund. She reportedly gave money to a Martha's Vineyard community center, the Little Brothers of the Poor in Chicago, and a South Dakota Indian Reservation—charities in which John had taken an interest. In 1990, Judy Belushi remarried, a writer-producer named Victor Pisano. Then it was out with the old and in with the new in an auction to benefit the memorial foundation, she told reporters. Among the items that were expected to fetch upward of $500,000: Belushi's 1965 Volvo, his drum set, an autographed photo of B. B. King, and fan portraits of Belushi as a killer bee, a Samurai warrior, and as a vastly overweight Elizabeth Taylor.

Why dispose of John's things at such a late date? Simple, said Judy. It was time to bury the past. Besides, a lot of the items were becoming mildewed.

Yul Brynner

THE GYPSIES OF EUROPE LIVE BY A COMMON rule for the road. When it comes to surviving among non-gypsies, steal only what you need for today. The actor Yul Brynner, who prided himself—falsely—as something of a gypsy king, didn't steal, however, and, at the end of his life, had accumulated more than he needed for several lifetimes.

Like a man driven, Brynner worked like a slave up to within months of the day he succumbed to lung cancer, earning millions of dollars he would never have the opportunity to spend. Like the belligerent, headstrong ruler he portrayed in the musical *The King and I*, a role with which his name became synonymous, it seems Brynner was determined to go out in a blaze of glory. He did, and then again, he didn't. He walked off the stage in triumph but only to walk directly into his grave. And although he finished his life having to be grateful to many people, he remembered virtually none of them in his will.

Brynner was born in Vladivostok, in Asian Soviet Russia, July 11, 1920, and moved to Paris with his mother and sister after his father abandoned them for the company of a beautiful younger woman. In Paris his mother lost complete control of Yul when he discovered the magnetic effect his exotic looks and manly swagger had on the opposite sex. Women literally threw themselves at him.

Brynner fell in with a group of gypsies, worked in Russian restaurants as a musical performer, and finally joined a circus. At the age of sixteen he set himself a goal: to become a movie star by the time he was thirty. He did that, and much more: "His hunger for triumph was so fierce and tireless that anything less than stardom was unimaginable." So wrote his only son, Rock, in 1989.

After a brief detour to China where he traveled with his father and stepmother, Brynner moved to America to study acting in Connecticut with Michael Chekhov, the son of the great dramatist Anton. Brynner was soon working in nightclubs and at private parties in New York, singing and strumming a gypsy seven-string guitar. He met his first wife, actress Virginia Gilmore, at one such gig in 1942; they quickly burst into the gossip columns as "Virginia Gilmore and some gypsy she met in New York." Soon they had a son, Rock, and moved into a Manhattan apartment over a dry cleaner's.

At first the Brynners lived hand-to-mouth, in part because the head of the household liked to live extravagantly. "I have no respect for money at all," he told Virginia. "I piss on it." Virginia did come to enjoy some early success in theater, but she soon began to slide into obscurity, especially compared to the phenomenal rise of her self-styled gypsy.

For Yul's career flowered quickly. In 1951 he appeared onstage for the first time as the imperious yet uncertain Siamese monarch in Richard Rodgers and Oscar Hammerstein II's *The King and I*. Brynner defined the role; and then, over the years, the role defined Brynner. The critic Brooks Atkinson wrote in *The New York Times* that Brynner's "vehement, restless, keen-minded King is a terse and vivid characterization with a blazing spirit and stylized ruthlessness of manners and makeup." As Brynner's life progressed, he increasingly transformed himself into the character he had created. By the time he died, his own "ruthlessness of manners" would take a cruel turn.

Although the show was a hit on Broadway for three years running, the marriage was failing. Virginia renounced her acting career and began drinking. Brynner, meanwhile, had never lost his appetite for sexual variety, and, as he would during all four of his marriages, began having affairs. The infidelity—and the scale on which it existed—seemed in line with the rest of Brynner's compulsions. He loved, spent, worked, played, and smoked cigarettes with the intensity of a Roman candle.

"What drives me," he once said, "is not compulsion. It's more because of something someone once said of me: 'Yul was born with an extra quart of champagne in his blood.' " Once, while water-skiing on Long Island Sound, Brynner sustained a serious scalp wound (he was balding from an early age, but shaved the rest off for *The King and I*, and kept his head totally shorn thereafter). Rather than stopping his skiing to have the wound tended by a doctor, Brynner had a friend hold a mirror while he himself sewed two stitches with a fishhook and nylon line. Then he resumed skiing.

In 1958 Brynner fell in love with a singer who bore him a daughter they named Lark. He was divorced from his first wife of ˉfifteen years soon after, although he did not marry Lark's mother. Without skipping very many beats he married Doris Kleiner, a high-society Chilean of Yugoslavian parentage whom he had met in Paris. She was ten years younger than he, and they set up house in Switzerland, where Brynner had moved, in part to escape paying U.S. income taxes. With this union Brynner's lifestyle began to change, to suit his new wife's old-money background. He collected fine art, accumulating a collection that included two Picassos and a Cézanne. In 1962 she bore him a daughter whom they named Victoria; but by 1968 that marriage also was on the rocks. He was now infatuated with a high-society Parisian, Jacqueline de Croisset. They married in 1971, settling in Normandy in an elaborate old château. Unable to have children of their own, they adopted two Vietnamese orphans, Mia and Melody.

Ironically, just as his domestic life seemed to settle down, his career was running out of gas. There was an attempt to launch a television series based on *The King and I,* but that flopped. He made a number of forgettable films, and even his one hit, *Westworld,* proved undistinguished. What followed were several theater productions but they were not moneymakers.

Finally, in 1977 at the age of 56, Brynner reappeared as his most famous creation, in a Broadway revival of *The King and I.* The show and he were a huge hit all over again, as women who'd fallen in love with him in the 1950s came out in droves to relive their youth—and this time bring along their daughters.

"Mr. Brynner," one reviewer wrote, "appears to be in a

state of eternally lean, trim fitness." The show ran for a year and a half, and then, because his expenses remained so high and the role was the only vehicle suitable to both his salary demands and his ego, Brynner settled into a long, difficult routine of playing the King of Siam on the road, all across America, in England, in Europe, and back again.

But these were not to be his golden years.

"To maintain [this lifestyle], he was condemned to wander the earth, playing King," his son revealed. "He lived out the [last eight] years of his life on the perpetual treadmill of eight shows a week. He loved his stardom, but he hated his life. There was nothing he could do to escape, and he resented everyone around him for the trap he was in."

Meanwhile, his own body was beginning to show its disrespect for the King. Brynner had had a pre-cancerous growth removed from his vocal cords in the mid-1970s, and actually lost his voice for three weeks during rehearsals for the initial revival of *The King and I*. He had developed pain in his spine and legs; sadly, he could barely walk a city block. Yet somehow he managed to draw himself together and perform as though nothing were wrong. He refused to allow himself a rest. He once told his son Rock, "Nothing could be worse than a lingering death, bedridden and kept alive by doctors. It's probably the only thing in the world I'm really afraid of. Personally, I would take care of business well before that. I want to feel my bones being crushed and taste the blood in my mouth."

As he headed out for his eighth year on the road with *The King and I,* his marriage to Jacqueline unraveled. His increasingly dictatorial and mean-spirited behavior, plus the rigors of living on the road, had taken their toll.

In 1983, he married his last wife, a dancer in her twenties from the London production of the show. She called herself Kathy Lee, but her real name was Kathy Yam Choo. That same year he learned that he had inoperable lung cancer. Radiation therapy ensued, and the Brynner stamina—even if it was only a façade—proved itself once more. He publicly announced that he was cured.

But in the winter of 1984 he began the "farewell tour" of the road show, followed by a four-month run on Broadway. "I couldn't see myself going to bed and waiting to see what would happen with my illness," he told a reporter. "I preferred to play to 2,000 or 3,000 people and standing ovations. The choice is quite simple."

By the time that last revival of the show opened on Broadway, in January 1985, Brynner had alienated almost all the people who had mattered to him during the earlier stages of his life. Surrounded by newcomers, he demanded from them and everyone else a steady flow of undiluted praise. Meanwhile, the pains in his body became sharper and sharper, until his co-star had to almost carry him through a polka they did to the tune "Shall We Dance?" The show closed finally on June 30, 1985. Yul Brynner had played the king 4,633 times.

The very next morning he signed a new draft of his will, leaving most of his estate to his new wife, Kathy Lee, and naming his lawyer, Michael Lynne, as co-executor. He left Kathy their New York co-op at United Nations Plaza (which she sold three years after his death for what friends estimated to be $1.75 million), "together with all furniture and furnishings therein and all policies of insurance related thereto." He also left her a "life estate" in his French château and "all of my right, title, and interest in the Property which does not pass on my death to my children under the laws of France."

"I have intentionally made no provision," the will stated, "for any of my children not named in this Will."

Two months later, in September, he suffered a stroke, possibly triggered by medication he was taking, and began a long, horrible, month-long slide toward death. For all his blustering, Brynner died the death he had feared most.

Brynner left his son Rock some stock he owned in the trendy restaurant chain, the Hard Rock Café. He also left Rock and daughter Victoria $50,000 each; a $100,000 trust for Victoria; and $25,000 to his illegitimate daughter Lark. Yet he was seen to have practically disinherited them all, in light of the money he had made. Rock was especially bitter in his memoirs, published in 1989. "To the maximum extent usually allowed by the courts, he had written everyone out of his will and left his entire estate to the young dancing girl he married twenty-nine months earlier," his only son complained.

Brynner earned an estimated $20 million in his career, as much as five million from *The King and I* alone. He left some of his art to his lawyer and a friend, but "not even a memento for his own children," his son said. The will did provide for the futures of Mia and Melody, the Vietnamese children he had adopted, by setting up a trust for them and designating them as heirs if Kathy Lee were to die.

Kathy Lee and Jacqueline, his third wife with whom he adopted the Vietnamese children, got into a legal battle over proceeds of an insurance payment. But, according to friends of Kathy, that skirmish ended when Jacqueline simply gave up, since Kathy intended to fight her every step of the way. Attorneys for Mia and Melody did win a settlement from the estate, almost $500,000.

Typically, it was Brynner the King who enjoyed the last word—not only to those he gifted or slighted in his will, but to those adoring fans who fueled his imperious ego. After his death, Brynner appeared in a pre-recorded television commercial he had done for the American Cancer Society. He warned all his loyal subjects not to smoke.

Truman Capote

UNQUESTIONABLY ONE OF AMERICA'S MOST brilliant writers, Truman Capote was also one of this country's most unrepentant bitchy boys of letters when he died on August 25, 1984. Estate tax papers list him as having died a single man and the only person named as a beneficiary of his estate is John Paul Dunphy, whose "relationship to decedent" is given coldly as "none."

Nothing could be further from the truth. "Jack" Dunphy was Capote's longtime friend, companion and, when they were much younger, lover. In fact, Capote's will is quite sentimental. He also left a trust fund in memory of the other literary romance of his life.

When Capote died at the age of sixty, of complications from drug and alcohol abuse, Dunphy was a relatively invisible part of Capote's public life, by his own design. Dunphy, also a writer, had lived for years in a house the two shared in

Sagaponack, New York, a quiet seaside community at the eastern end of Long Island. Dunphy avoided the high-society, celebrity-filled life on which Capote seemed to thrive.

Born on a Tuesday, September 30, 1924, Truman Streckfus Persons was an unwelcome addition to his teenaged mother's life. She had meant to have an abortion, feeling she had married the wrong man and wasn't ready to settle down, but she waited too long, and was forced to have the baby against her better judgment. She and Truman's father moved around quite a bit in his first years, locking up the child in their hotel room while they went to work or else to socialize (his mother also had affairs with dozens of men). His parents finally dropped off Truman, at the age of six, with relatives in Monroeville, Alabama; after which his mother divorced his father and married one Joe Capote, whose last name Truman took. Mr. and Mrs. Capote moved to New York and when Truman was a teenager coming into his own as a precocious writer, he joined them.

Capote was not only a singular literary talent, but also a keen wit and a hotly pursued dinner companion. He led a fantastically rich life socially as well as professionally. In the late 1940s he was a literary child star, published in *The New Yorker* as a teenager and selling his first novel, *Other Voices, Other Rooms,* at the age of twenty-two for an advance of $20,000 ($125,000 in 1990 dollars).

The crowning achievement of his career is generally considered to be *In Cold Blood,* his 1966 non-fiction account of the brutal 1959 murder of a Kansas farm family by two drifters, which in 1967 was made into a hit film. He also wrote screenplays, stage plays, poetry, and many short stories, and, at one time or another, knew practically every major literary light in his contemporary universe.

Capote died leaving an estate valued at about $2.3 million, although it continues to earn royalties from his books and films. His will was short, six typewritten pages, and, aside from bequests, contained mostly boilerplate legal language. He left all of his personal property and real estate, including the house at Sagaponack, to Jack Dunphy, and set up an annual annuity of nearly $100,000 for him from a trust fund established with the balance of the proceeds of his estate.

Upon Dunphy's death, the income from the trust fund was to be used to establish a prize or prizes for excellence in literary criticism in memory of Capote's other great literary affair, with Newton Arvin. Capote wanted the "Truman Capote Award for Literary Criticism in Memory of Newton Arvin" to be administered by a college or university or, if no college or university would take it on, that the income be used to provide literary scholarships.

Capote had claimed several very close friends who were women, including Joanne Carson, who was with him when he died. But effeminate in his mannerisms from an early age, and considered pretty as a child and young man, Capote apparently never entertained the notion of adopting a child, let alone trying to father one, and died without a natural heir.

The two great loves of Capote's life could not have been more different. Newton Arvin and he met in 1946 at Yaddo, a writers' retreat in Saratoga Springs, where Capote had gone to work on his first novel. Arvin was a professor of literature at Smith College in Massachusetts and a deeply closeted homosexual who attempted suicide several times and, in the early 1960s, was arrested for owning a huge quantity of homoerotic pornography. He was forty-five, bald, wore glasses, was retiring, anemic, and suffered frequent bouts of depression, vertigo, and other psychological maladies. He has been described as the quintessential "mousy college professor." Capote, on the other hand, was twenty-two, dynamic, attractive, and, with his spell-binding storytelling abilities, had captivated the fifteen or twenty other writers who were working at Yaddo that summer.

But opposites have been known to attract; two days after Arvin and Capote's paths crossed, they began a passionate romance that lasted about three years. Capote once described Arvin as "a charming person, cultivated in every way, with the most wonderfully subtle mind. He was like a lozenge that you could keep turning to the light, one way or another, and the most beautiful colors would come out."

Their relationship fizzled after a couple of years when Capote, returning from a trip to Europe, discovered that Arvin had been carrying on an affair with one of Capote's best friends. Still, they remained on good terms up until Arvin's death in March 1963 of cancer.

Capote met Jack Dunphy in 1948. Dunphy was everything Arvin was not: he was thirty-four (ten years Capote's senior), Irish and feisty, handsome and vital. He had receding red hair, was an ex-dancer, had written a novel, and had been married to Joan McCracken, a Broadway musical comedy star who later married Bob Fosse. He also had never had a physical relationship with a man. He'd had fantasies, it was said, but hadn't acted on them until his wife ran off with another man and he turned against women forever.

Jack Dunphy was Truman's rock. "He is the only person I trust one hundred percent," Capote once said. "He is everything to me. He is not my shadow. He is not my alter ego. He is the one person I will love until the day I die."

Capote undoubtedly did love Dunphy until the day he died, although the relationship began to unravel in the late '60s. According to Capote, Dunphy insisted on leaving New York, as he did every year, to spend time in Verbier, Switzerland, where they owned a condominium, only this time Dunphy wanted to stay there.

The two men had always led lives of their own apart from the relationship. Now they started to drift apart further, with each having his own affairs, until the sex between them ceased altogether. Capote and Dunphy thereafter became companions and old friends. "It was unthinkable that we would ever break up," Dunphy once said. "People thought our relationship was based on sex. It wasn't."

Capote had been a heavy drinker much of his life, but in the 1970s he began to go downhill. The pace of his decline accelerated in the next decade, after the society crowd in which he moved rejected him for writing a cover story for *Esquire* magazine (which later formed part of a book, *Answered Prayers*), "La Côte Basque, 1965," after the French restaurant where the doyennes of society mingled at lunch. The gossipy piece exposed the inner circle to ridicule as Truman betrayed several confidences in scorching, thinly veiled anecdotes. Capote was perceived as having bitten the hands that had been feeding him all those years. Finding himself isolated, he drank more, used increased dosages of drugs adjusted to his moods, and took to spending more and more time in hospitals recovering from his binges.

Old friends and acquaintances began to avoid him, mystified at his self-destruction. Alan Schwartz, a Manhattan lawyer retained by Capote in the early 1970s and later named executor of Capote's estate, said, "I recognized finally that he really was killing himself." On May 4, 1981, at the United Nations Plaza apartment where he had lived for many years, Capote signed his last will and testament, and began the final slide that would end in his death three years later.

Near the end he suffered from phlebitis, a potentially fatal inflammation of the veins, that swelled his left leg. He developed blood clots in his lungs. Dunphy, concerned, returned from Verbier.

Capote suffered two bad falls in the first weeks of 1984, after which he was in and out of the hospital. He managed to quit drinking long enough for the phlebitis to go into remission, only to start drinking again. Finally he agreed to check into a rehabilitation clinic near Philadelphia. But by this time Dunphy was apparently burned out on Capote's suicide wishes. The friend refused to help Capote pack, refused to see him—yet he drove him into New York to catch a connecting ride to the clinic. Capote, crushed at Dunphy's meanness, called him a "monster."

On August 23, 1984, Capote was released from the clinic. He retreated from New York to visit Joanne Carson, ex-wife of *Tonight Show* host Johnny Carson, at her home in Los Angeles. Joanne was one of Capote's most devoted friends and herself a bit of a social misfit. They'd met shortly after publication of *In Cold Blood* and something clicked; Joanne became Capote's project when she divorced Johnny and was ostracized by the entertainment community.

"She's a bore and a pain in the ass," Capote once confided to a friend. "But I feel sorry for her and I like her." In return, Joanne mothered him.

When he arrived in Los Angeles, on a Thursday, he told Joanne, "It's all over with Jack. Fini." Two days later, Joanne went to wake her houseguest at 7:30 in the morning. Capote looked so ill she wanted to call a doctor, but he held her hand and made her sit with him. Joanne would later say they talked for several hours. Capote dredged up memories of his youth as the life leaked out of him, recalling his six-year-old's desire to leave Alabama and fly to China. He grew weaker and weaker until, just before noon, he said, "I'm cold," and died.

Of Capote's estate, which included a number of stock and bond investments, Dunphy's inheritance for tax purposes was valued at $572,921.49, which included the Verbier condominium. He was seventy years old at the time; in the calculation of his total inheritance he was to receive an annual payment of $94,600. Tax filings also show that personal papers and manuscripts valued at almost $205,000 were donated to the New York Public Library. A total of $1.4 million was placed in a charitable trust to pay the income to Dunphy until his death, after which the funds were to be turned over toward the literary criticism prizes.

Funeral and administration expenses ate up $207,000, and Capote left debts of $124,000, including $3,781.78 to Joanne Carson for money she had advanced the mortuary. Capote died owing money to a dozen or so hospitals and doctors, and a few New York restaurants . . . including $131.20 to La Côte Basque.

Joan Crawford

HOLLYWOOD'S GOLDEN ERA SUPERSTAR JOAN Crawford authored one of the most famous wills of all time, thanks to her adopted daughter, Christina, born in 1939. Who knows whether "Tina," as Joan called her, would have been compelled to spill the beans if Joan, or "The Bitch," as Christina called her, had not been so mean.

Crawford signed her will about six months before she expired of a heart attack on May 10, 1977, the Tuesday after Mother's Day. She was sixty-nine, or maybe a few years older. Among other characteristics, Joan Crawford lied about her age.

Crawford knew she was dying when she signed the will. She hadn't seen a doctor in about eighteen months, in part because she was a practitioner of Christian Science, a religion that eschews traditional medical care. But she was also reportedly terrified to find out what was really wrong with her, as for some time she'd been losing weight and experiencing severe back pain. (Only later was it determined that she was suffering with cancer.) Once a publicity hound, Crawford turned recluse in her last couple of years, since the moment she had seen a particularly hideous press picture of herself at a 1974 party. Not only was Crawford out of focus and caught in the most unflattering glare of the photographer's flash, but she looked bloated—no doubt a byproduct of the steady diet of straight vodka she had consumed for the last twenty-five years of her life—and she was wearing a curly old-lady's wig that looked as if it had been plopped on her head as an afterthought.

"I'm never going out in public again," she vowed. It was indeed her last public appearance.

Instead, Crawford stayed holed up in her small Manhattan apartment on East 69th Street. She'd moved out of the white plastic palace she'd helped her last husband, Pepsi-Cola president Alfred Steele, build on Fifth Avenue. Then she was forced to move again, to even tinier quarters in the same building. Now she shrank her world further, staying indoors, sending her housekeeper or friends out for food and other necessities, keeping in touch with the outside world via telephone, visits from friends, her extensive correspondence, or else watching television. She was a ferocious letter writer, some months sending out as many as 10,000 notes to Pepsi dealers, TV stars she admired, friends and, of course, fans. She would sometimes arise at five in the morning to start her missives.

Born Lucille LeSueur in San Antonio, Joan Crawford made more than eighty movies, playing roles that, in retrospect, uniquely suited her: a prostitute, a shopgirl, a sophisticate, a mother, a blackmailer, and a schizophrenic. She may not have qualified as a blackmailer, but there were elements of all the other roles lurking near the surface of her disturbed personality.

Although one of the top ten money-making actresses during the Depression, Crawford was also a big spender. Once she had learned to live like a movie queen, she never adjusted to leaner times—although she would often brag about her pre-star days as a waitress. She was falling behind in her bills in 1955 when she married Steele, a portly, bespectacled business executive with deep pockets, whom she treated with open disdain almost as soon as the ring was secured on her finger.

When Steele suddenly died of a heart attack in 1959, it was discovered that his pockets were not as deep as believed. Rising to the situation, Crawford made a successful power play for an active role at Pepsi, which she parlayed over the next twenty years into the sweetest of deals: a $50,000-a-year salary ($210,000 in 1990 dollars); $40,000-a-year expense account; a $1,500-a-month rent allowance; $12,000-a-year secretary; and $40-a-week allowance for a hairdresser. Pepsi retired her in 1974 when she turned sixty-five, at which point her life seemed to end, though she lived another three years.

Joan's relationship with Christina—and with her adopted son Christopher—is now legendary, but it wasn't clear at the time she died, except to a few privileged insiders. (Crawford apparently could not have children of her own, and adopted four children in her life. Christina was the eldest, Christopher was several years younger. When Christina was in high school, Joan adopted two little girls who, as it turned out, became the chief beneficiaries of her will.)

The clause in the will relating to Christina and Christopher made headlines in 1977: "It is my intention to make no provision herein for my son Christopher or my daughter Christina for reasons that are well-known to them."

The reasons certainly became well known to everybody with the 1978 publication of Christina's best-selling memoir,

Mommie Dearest. Besides being a manipulative, alcoholic, self-involved child-abuser of the first order (Crawford might be jailed on serious charges if she committed her acts today), Joan never forgave Christina for having a relatively innocuous sexual encounter, when she was only eleven, with a sixteen-year-old boy at the private school she attended.

When Joan heard about the incident she called her daughter a "common whore." Of all the horrors that Joan visited upon Christina—keeping her and Christopher awake all night scrubbing floors, the physical and emotional beatings—this name-calling seemed to damage their relationship most, and beyond repair. After that, Crawford seemed to regard Christina as competition, the way she viewed all women in her career and social life. She badgered Christina, faulted her whenever possible, and left her at school on weekends and holidays instead of allowing the girl to come home.

About the same time her relationship with Christina soured, Crawford also turned against Christopher with a vengeance. He was now all of eight years old, had ceased being a cuddly little boy, and had begun to show signs of his emerging manhood. She beat him, forced him to stay up all night doing housework, and tied him up to the corners of his bed.

"As I watched the hateful way Mother treated my brother," Christina wrote, "I realized for the first time that she really didn't like men." Joan had accumulated a coterie of gay men she considered her friends; and Christina would later discover that Joan had tried to seduce one of the maids.

Christina attempted to stick it out at school, in spite of the scandal her sexual encounter had caused. But a couple of years later Joan yanked her out for seeing an older boy who had been captain of the football team. A few days after Christina's return home, they argued and, in a drunken rage, Crawford tried to strangle Christina. Joan's secretary, hearing the ruckus, intervened and pulled mother off daughter, possibly saving the girl's life. When she turned fourteen, Christina was sent to a convent; communication from Crawford was dispatched mainly through short, cold notes on her professional stationery.

Christopher rebelled in typically boyish ways, getting himself thrown out of school for various infractions, and finally being sent to Juvenile Hall. He remained estranged from his adopted mother for the rest of his life, but Christina periodically came back for more abuse, trying fruitlessly to please her unsatisfiable mother.

Four years before she died, Crawford made her final appearance before an adoring audience of 1,500 fans at a special tribute in New York. Asked whether she would raise her children again the same way she had, she responded, "Yes. I believe the reason most kids are on pot and other junk is because they don't have enough love or discipline at home."

Crawford couldn't control either of the two eldest children and she cut them out of her will, if in fact they had ever been in it at any point. She died leaving an estate valued at about $1.3 million. All of her personal belongings went to Cathy Lalonde, the closer and more attentive of the two younger adopted children. Married and mothers themselves when *Mommie Dearest* was published, both Cathy and her sister Cynthia Crawford Jordan refused to accept Christina's view of their adopted mother. "Her twisted lies should not be given credence," they told the press. Joan left Cathy and Cynthia $77,500 each, though she still retained control of them even in death; her will stipulated that the money be paid out over thirty years.

The belongings of Joan Crawford—who reportedly owned 100 wigs—were sold off in January 1978 during three separate auctions. Among the items sold were a 300-piece costume jewelry collection that went for $6,500; 100 lots of fine gold jewelry; 85 pairs of false eyelashes that fetched $325; 200 pairs of custom-made shoes; her guest book for $12,800, the highest auction price; a blue and green stone bib necklace with matching bracelet and earrings for which Andy Warhol paid $150; an amethyst and diamond bangle purchased by director Ron Link for $2,500; monogrammed book matches, playing cards, writing paper, bed linens, and towels. *The San Francisco Examiner,* in itemizing the Crawford booty, noted a strange discovery: A storage closet in her apartment was found to contain some 200 cans of cleanser.

Joan left $5,000 each to the four children of Cathy and Cynthia, payable when they reached twenty-one.

She left similar small amounts to some of the people who had worked for her over the years as makeup and wardrobe people, as well as $5,000 to a devoted fan, Bernice Oshatz, who spent time taking care of Joan near the end of her life. (Crawford had often used fans as household help when she was down on her luck, or had worn out her welcome with employment agencies by firing everyone they sent her.) She also left $5,000 to a publicist friend, Michael Sean O'Shea.

The rest of her estate went to charities, some of which seemed odd choices for someone who was dying of cancer and was a practicing Christian Scientist, adamant against going to the doctor: the Muscular Dystrophy Association; the American Cancer Society; and the American Heart Association. Finally, she left shares of her estate to the USO and the Motion Picture Country House, a film industry retirement home.

Christina and Christopher, having fought their entire childhood for their self-respect and, at times, even their survival, were not about to let Joan off scot-free. They filed objections to the will, arguing that their mother was incompetent, her mind beclouded by booze and the pain of her illness, that she was being manipulated by their sister (Cathy Lalonde and her husband), and that Joan was suffering from a bad case of monomania which "was apparently based on the belief that [Christina] had desires on [Joan's] late husband, Alfred Steele, when [Joan] was married to him."

After plenty of legal pushing and shoving among the interested parties, an agreement was ultimately reached on June 5, 1979. Christina and Christopher would share $55,000, tax-free.

In addition, Cathy Lalonde agreed to give to Christina a lone memento of her relationship with her world-famous mother, a 1941 plaster bust of Joan that carried a simple inscription: "To Christina."

James Dean

THE ACTOR LIVED FAST AND DIED YOUNG—
only twenty-four, with his two most famous movies as yet
unreleased—but he didn't leave a very pretty corpse. James
Dean, at the very beginning of a spectacular film career, was
killed instantly on September 30, 1955, when the brand-new
silver Porsche he was driving to a racing meet in Salinas,
California, collided with another car, nearly severing Dean's
head. Ironically, shortly before being killed, the pouty, icono-
clastic symbol of rebellious youth had recorded a rather upbeat
advertisement for road safety. Its tag line, as spoken by Dean:
"Remember, the next life you save may be mine."

Dean's career and life were still being formed at the time
of the fatality, so it can hardly be considered surprising that the
young wanderer had not gotten around to writing a will. He
was far from being a stable family man; he had hardly any

family of his own at all. Considered, by most accounts, sexually ambivalent (graphic stories as well as photographs continue to circulate privately three and a half decades after his death), Dean was never married and left no children. The courts, therefore, named the father he rebelled against as his heir, lending a further mocking touch to the short, fast life of James Byron Dean.

Born February 8, 1931, in Marion, Indiana, the son of a dental technician, James Dean developed a screen image that required little honing by studio publicity machines. He *was* a social rebel, after having suffered a sad, disruptive childhood, due largely to his neglectful father Winton Dean.

At the age of five, James Dean moved to Los Angeles with his parents. When the boy's mother died three years later, Winton sent him to a farm in Iowa, to be raised by relatives. Ten years later, James returned to California on his own, to attend Santa Monica Junior College and UCLA. He soon began acting in a small theater group, and appearing in some television commercials. In 1951 and 1952, he played bits in the forgettable Hollywood movies *Sailor Beware, Fixed Bayonets, Has Anybody Seen My Gal,* and *Trouble Along the Way.* By early 1953, his compact, brooding figure could be spotted around New York, hanging around the Actors Studio. It was there, especially, that he developed the '50s style of young leading man: offbeat, moody, borderline inarticulate, yet strong enough a presence to land parts in two Broadway plays, *See the Jaguar* and *The Immoralist.* And impressive enough to capture the eye of a Warner Bros. talent scout, who took Dean back to Hollywood.

Dean's first movie starring role was in 1955's *East of Eden,* directed by Elia Kazan, based on a period novel by John

Steinbeck. The film, about an insecure son's fatalistic struggle to gain the respect of his unfeeling, overbearing father, catapulted the slinking screen presence into the very embodiment of the raging, anguished, alienated youth of his own era. So strong was Dean's persona that, with his powerful second starring role as Jim in 1955's *Rebel Without a Cause,* the actor practically appeared to be playing himself.

"I want answers *now*," he hollers at the picture's weak father, who easily could have been Winton Dean. "I'm not interested in what I'll understand ten years from now."

James Dean was already dead by the time *Rebel* hit the screen, followed the next year by the epic about rival Texas oil barons, *Giant,* based on the novel by Edna Ferber. Like his two previous films, this one dealt with a romantic sort of nonconformist forced to find his way in a world devoid of nobility, a hostile environment not of his own making.

According to court papers, Winton Dean was the only living relative at the time James Dean died that fateful day in September. It is not clear who, if anyone, receives the royalties from the endless array of posters, party plates, and postcards bearing the Dean likeness that have proliferated over the years. But it was Dean's father who inherited the personal possessions and small estate of the twenty-four-year-old deceased rebel.

After selling a few of his son's assets, such as his horse "Cisco" for $130, a 1955 Ford station wagon for $2,200, and his Triumph motorcycle for $500, and paying some of the amassed debts and legal bills, Winton Dean received $93,000 in cash (more than it may seem—roughly $520,800 in 1990 dollars), and several personal items from his son's estate. The money was due almost entirely to a $100,000 life insurance policy, for without it, there would have been practically nothing of value in the estate, except for the cachet attached to its sundry items for having once belonged to James Dean.

The list of Dean's personal effects reads, sadly, like the contents of a college junior's apartment. The only items related to his film career were pairs of silver spurs and silver cufflinks with an oil-well design—in all likelihood studio gifts in connection with his role as Elizabeth Taylor's unsuitable and unrequited romance in *Giant,* the film he had finished only a week before he slammed his Porsche into the other car.

Dean's other effects, turned over to his father, included:

One Le Coultre watch with a black face and gold
   dial
One silver I.D. bracelet
Four sportscar racing trophies
One white clay mask of Dean's face
One Marlin .22 caliber rifle
One drawing board
Three slabs of unfinished wood used for a table top
Various pieces of luggage
One electric blanket
One white plaster of paris statuette of Apollo
One set of small bongo drums
One "large pile of clothes"
One GI duffel bag
. . . and the list goes on for several pages.

James Dean's legacy bloomed almost immediately upon his death. Cults sprang up, many of the members resolutely refusing to believe that their idol was dead, and the James Dean mystique was firmly established. By the 1970s, and throughout the '80s and seemingly into the '90s, the denim-clad figure and rebellious nature of James Dean transmuted him—along with Marilyn Monroe, who seven years later was also to die too suddenly and too young—into a definitive pop-culture icon.

Jack Dempsey

HIS FAME AS A BOXER LASTED FOR ALMOST
sixty years after he lost his seven-year grip on the world's
heavyweight title, showing he had clearly captured the imagina-
tions of more than one generation of fight fans. Yet, when he
died, Jack Dempsey was remembered as a gentle and generous
man.

William Harrison Dempsey was born in Manassa, Colorado, in 1895, worked in mining camps, and began boxing as
a way to pick up a few extra dollars. He had a series of
nicknames along the way—Kid Blackie and the Manassa
Mauler (the one that stuck)—but settled on Jack Dempsey, a
name his brother Bernie used as a boxer, when he substituted
for Bernie in the ring one night and won. By the time Jack got
to his first "world" match at the age of twenty-four, he'd
fought more than eighty professional bouts, and had twenty-
one first-round knockouts to his credit.

Dempsey's name endured over the decades partly because, in his first championship fight in 1919, he destroyed in three dramatic, exciting rounds a man who was five inches taller and almost sixty pounds heavier. Another reason is that this fight—against Jess Willard, in which Willard was down seven times before he was knocked out—was immortalized in a powerful oil painting by Montgomery Flagg. It showed Dempsey in the ring, a towering mass of muscle and sweat, standing over the flattened Willard before a roaring crowd of men in period hats. The painting captured forever the moment of raw, undistracted violence and victory in Dempsey's face, to say nothing of the spirited atmosphere of the Roaring Twenties.

Dempsey lost his title in 1926 to Gene Tunney in a decision that many in the boxing world called the "long count" and thought was grossly unfair. He had already lost one bout with Tunney when, in a rematch, he knocked Tunney out. Dempsey mistakenly stood over his opponent instead of going to a neutral corner as the referee began the count. The referee stopped, told Dempsey to go to his corner, then started the count all over again, giving Tunney enough time to gather his wits and get back on his feet. Tunney ended up the victor.

Dempsey's popularity continued to rise after he retired. He opened a restaurant in New York, named after himself, and was often there to autograph menus or pose for pictures with patrons. An Associated Press poll in 1950 named him the greatest fighter of the first half of the twentieth century and, in 1954, he was elected to the Boxing Hall of Fame.

He was married three times and had two daughters by his third wife, Hannah Williams. His fourth wife, Deanna Oiatelli, was with him when he died, in 1983, at the age of eighty-eight. He was buried in Southampton, New York, a wealthy beach enclave near New York.

Dempsey left all of his personal belongings and furniture to Deanna, and willed property he owned in San Bernardino, California, to his daughters. The rest of the estate was split up into thirds, among his wife and his two daughters. He took note in the will that, in case Deanna died before him, her daughter—his stepdaughter—would receive "all bric-a-brac and the Oriental screen, consisting of six panels, which were given to her by her father, now deceased."

The estate, for tax purposes, was valued at $517,000, and its most famous item, the Montgomery Flagg painting that Dempsey owned, was left to the Smithsonian Institution, which had been displaying it since 1983.

Perry Ellis

IN WHAT IS ARGUABLY THE MOST PRETEN-
tious business in the world, Perry Ellis sold a distinctly American design: it married traditional Ivy League clothes to the
breezy lifestyle of the 1970s and early '80s. The fashion industry called it the slouch look, and it turned Ellis into a very rich
man.

By contrast, Ellis's private life was not so traditional.
Although considered a homosexual, about the time he realized
he was probably dying of AIDS he legally contracted to create
an heir by talking a woman friend into having his child—a
daughter, as it happened, who, with little or no memory of her
father, inherited the bulk of his tremendous fortune.

Ellis's star was extinguished just as it was burning bright-
est. His last eight years were the period of his greatest success,
in his personal life as well as his business, leading right up to
the time he died in May 1986. He was born March 3, 1940,

the only son of an upper-middle-class Portsmouth, Virginia, couple. His father, a draftsman in the Norfolk naval dockyards, started his own fuel business, while his mother Winifred liked to take Perry shopping for clothes and dress him up. Perry enjoyed it even more than she did, and was later to say that some of his best childhood memories were the smells, sights, and sounds of department stores.

He joined the Coast Guard to avoid getting drafted during the Vietnam War, and managed to finagle his way onto the White House Honor Guard. Once discharged, he went to New York University, earned a Master's degree in retailing, and entered the employ of a department store company in Virginia.

In the early 1970s he worked as a stylist for a sportswear company in Connecticut. Ellis really got his career going in 1977 with the backing of Manhattan Industries, and thereafter it took him only five years to become one of the top American designers, despite his having had no formal training and no technical skills. What Ellis did possess was a unique sensitivity to what women were looking for in clothes; he also knew how to "work" the fashion press into giving his lines the maximum amount of exposure. His designs were considered fresh and exciting, not just a reworking of someone else's ideas, as was common with other designers. Not that everyone liked his lines. As one critic beefed, "[H]e designs for boys . . . not women who have breasts and hips."

Ellis freely wove his romantic life into his business life, but it was covert as far as the public was concerned. He was a social climber and snob, according to at least one biographer—attracted to bright, handsome, WASPish, Ivy League types, the kind of men seen in fashion ads. In the early 1970s he had taken up with Robert McDonald, a young man in the film business. They were lovers for six years, until 1980, when Ellis met the real love of his life, a contact that ultimately resulted in Ellis's death. Laughlin Barker was a handsome lawyer. Upon being introduced through a mutual friend, the two men hit it off immediately first on a romantic level, and soon afterward in business. Barker joined Ellis's company officially in 1982, at a time when it was earning about $60 million a year in licensing fees. Within three and a half years Barker had increased the bottom line fivefold.

Ellis would later say of Laughlin that he was "an extraordinary man and I loved him. We worked together twenty-four hours a day, and he brought genius and humor to this business. We were together five years, and there was never an argument or disagreement. I felt complete when he was here."

Sadly, by 1984 Barker was sick, dying of AIDS. So was Ellis, although he wasn't as far gone. At about the same time Ellis decided he wanted to leave a child. He broached the subject to a friend, Barbara Gallagher, who had been close to Ellis's ex-lover Robert McDonald, and was a freelance film producer and screenwriter. Presumably by *in vitro* fertilization, she became pregnant and, in the fall of 1984, gave birth to a girl they named Tyler Alexandra Gallagher Ellis. Ellis was present for the delivery, and he bought mother and child a home in California.

Meanwhile, Ellis and Barker grew much sicker. Barker died first, in January 1986. By this time Ellis, who was paying less attention to the company, had brought into the business Robert McDonald, his ex-lover, who would become president of Perry Ellis International, Incorporated. It was clear to everyone in the fashion business that Ellis was soon doomed to die of AIDS, but the company vigorously denied it and the fashion press largely ignored it, even though Ellis appeared at a couple of public functions looking nothing less than cadaverous. Even after he died, the company disputed that the cause was AIDS. The official statements cited the cause of death as viral encephalitis, a frequent byproduct of AIDS.

Ellis put the finishing touches on his will on January 27, 1986, a few weeks after Barker's death and four months before his own. On May 8, 1986, he slipped into a coma. His last words, a response to a comment from a visitor on the forest of flowers that surrounded his hospital bed, were, "Never enough."

Ellis's exact testamentary wishes are a mystery, because the will was set up in such a way that his assets existed in a blind trust, with his daughter as the principal beneficiary. His first request was to be cremated and the ashes sent to his mother in Norfolk for burial in the family plot.

To his mother he left property that they owned jointly, free and clear. This included property Ellis had inherited from his father. The rest of his assets he left in a revocable trust: houses, stock in the company, cash, and personal belongings. He left Robert McDonald in charge of the trust; the only beneficiaries were his daughter, his mother, and McDonald. One of his houses, on Water Island in Long Island Sound, was sold for a reported $800,000, and his Manhattan townhouse, for $4.35 million. He left an estate that was generating an estimated $10 million a year in income alone, suggesting assets in the neighborhood of $100 million.

On the company front, Perry Ellis International at the time of his death was grossing an estimated $750 million in annual retail sales. Industry watchdogs focused an eagle eye to see how it would fare without its namesake. The company hobbled along at first, then landed on sure footing. But in the immediate wake of the passing of its founder, his death was partially compensated for by the cashing-in of a corporate life insurance policy the business had taken out on Perry Ellis. It paid $5 million.

And what, ultimately, could be the legacy bequeathed Tyler Alexandra Gallagher Ellis? Perry Ellis presumably didn't know in 1983 that the AIDS virus was transmitted in semen, but, according to Jonathan Moor in his posthumous biography of the designer, it is possible that the child and mother could lead normal healthy lives. Moor quotes medical experts who believe that the chances of the mother and child getting the virus are probably small because, with *in vitro* fertilization, it is the pure sperm that is used and not the infected fluids that carry the virus.

Bob Fosse

GENEROSITY WAS AS COMMON TO HIM AS THE jut of a hip and the tilt of a bowler hat. A friend once said of dancer-choreographer-director Bob Fosse, "He was an inveterate check grabber all his life." When he died, Fosse earmarked special money to pick up the check one last time. His will provided $25,000 for sixty-six of his friends to go out and "have dinner on me. They all have at one time or other during my life been very kind to me. I thank them."

His will listed the addresses of those to be invited, and the guests included E. L. Doctorow, the writer; Ben Gazzara, the actor; Melanie Griffith, the actress; Buddy Hackett; Dustin Hoffman; Jessica Lange; Janet Leigh; Liza Minnelli; Roy Scheider; Gene Shalit, the critic; and Ben Vereen. The dinner was held at Tavern on the Green on October 30, 1987. Roy Scheider, who played the Fosse character in the largely autobiographical 1979 film *All That Jazz,* said, "It was as if he was orchestrating it . . . like another one of his spectaculars. Everybody was dancing. I don't think there was a dry body in the house."

Fosse, one of the last great stage choreographers, was born in Chicago on June 23, 1927, and at nine years old was already dreaming of becoming the next Fred Astaire. When he was ten, Fosse wrote to ask his idol what shoe size he wore. When, years later, Fosse met Astaire on the MGM lot, the young hoofer could not budge for nearly an hour, he was so overwhelmed.

Entering vaudeville at thirteen, Fosse wound up in New York at the age of twenty, worked as a chorus boy, and then formed a dance team with his first wife, Mary Ann Niles. He developed a unique dance style that had its roots in jazz; he dressed it with a bowler slanted over the eye, a white glove, a smooth roll of the shoulder, and a stiletto heel slicing the air. He himself always wore a funereal black, and invariably had a cigarette dangling out of his mouth.

Fosse developed a sense of his mortality early on. As a youngster he had imagined that he would be dead by age twenty-five. "It was romantic," he admitted later. "People would mourn me: 'Oh, that young career.'" As a result, he drove himself hard, abetted by cocaine and speed. In 1974 he suffered a massive heart attack, followed by open heart surgery. After that he cut down on the drugs but not the pace: smoking, womanizing, overworking, and eating rich foods remained Fosse's habits of choice.

Fosse's Broadway directorial credits included *Pippin, Chicago,* and *Dancin',* and, all told, he won ten Tony awards for his stage work. His movies were *Sweet Charity, Cabaret, Lenny, All That Jazz,* and *Star 80.* In *The Guinness Book of World Records* it is noted that he was the first person to win the triple crown of entertainment—a Tony for *Pippin,* an Oscar for *Cabaret,* and an Emmy for TV's *Liza with a Z*—all in one year, 1972.

All That Jazz, probably his best film and certainly his most personal (despite its splashy, self-indulgent musical numbers), dealt with his own death in a romantic vein that echoed his feelings as a young man. On film his character's demise is staged as a sardonic production number titled *Bye Bye Life.* "I like—not exactly sad, but melancholy endings," Fosse said. "They seem more true to life."

His death at the age of sixty, on the other hand, was true to theater. En route to the Washington, D.C., opening of a revival of *Sweet Charity,* he was seized by a massive heart attack. The show, as he would have wanted it, went on.

Fosse left an estate worth almost $4.5 million, the bulk of it to be divided between his daughter, Nicole, and his wife and collaborator of thirty years, the actress-dancer Gwen Verdon, even though they were legally separated at the time. The couple had remained close and she was at his side when he died. He left gifts of $7,000 to $20,000 each to his sister, one of his three ex-wives, his assistant, and several friends; $15,000 to the Heart Fund of New York; and $15,000 to the Post Graduate Center for Mental Health.

To his agent, Samuel Cohn, he left his interest in a restaurant called The Laundry in the resort of East Hampton, Long Island, New York, where Fosse owned a summer house.

Fosse also set up a student fund with $100,000. The Bob Fosse Theatre Scholarship would, as long as his executors Verdon and daughter Nicole were alive, provide "financial assistance to deserving individuals for their education and training in the theatrical arts."

As Fosse wrote, "I have been motivated to establish this

fund because my life has been devoted to the American theater and its continued well-being and improvement are of great importance to me. It is my intention in establishing this fund to provide an opportunity for talented individuals to obtain training for their careers in the theater which might not otherwise be available to them, and thereby, through the contributions which they will make in their careers, enhance and improve the quality of theater in the United States."

Clark Gable

WILLIAM CLARK GABLE, BORN FEBRUARY 1, 1901, didn't give a damn—about children, anyway. His will specifically disinherited anyone who came forward claiming to be his heir. After all, as the will stated, "I have no children." This was in spite of years of stories to the contrary.

Then, just five months before he died in 1960, Gable's fifth wife announced that she was pregnant and the movies' Rhett Butler was finally going to become a father—legitimately. Gable was in the middle of working on *The Misfits* with Marilyn Monroe, and the news apparently made him giddy. He told anyone who would listen that he hoped the child would be a son and that he could finally retire to devote himself to raising the boy.

Fate, however, took a bizarre twist. The King of Hollywood, as he was known, died of a heart attack soon after filming ended, and never got to see the boy whom his wife,

Kathleen G. Gable, bore him four months later. Neither did he have the opportunity to change his will. He left just about everything to Kathleen, with the exception of a piece of North Hollywood property measuring fifty by one hundred feet. This he left to one of his former wives, Josephine Dillon. It isn't clear what the estate was worth when Gable died, but nine years later, in a court filing associated with the estate, attorneys listed almost $3.5 million in assets and income.

Gable's will was contested by a woman who claimed Gable had promised to include her in his will, to acknowledge his guilt at having contributed to her husband's death. The story was somewhat convoluted, and had to do with the death of Gable's most famous wife, the beloved actress Carole Lombard. She had toured on a war bond rally in January 1942, and Gable had urged her publicity agent, Otto Winkler, to accompany her. Winkler opted not to go, according to his wife, but Gable insisted.

On the last leg of their journey, from Las Vegas, the plane crashed, killing both Lombard and Winkler. According to Winkler's widow, Gable was broken up about the tragedy, and said "he felt he was to blame for [Otto's] death, having been the one who persuaded him to go with Carole Lombard."

Otto's widow, Jill Winkler Rath (she had remarried), announced she was going to sue the airline company for her husband's death, but claimed Gable convinced her otherwise, saying he did not wish to be dragged into court and have to deal with Lombard's relatives. To keep Winkler from filing her lawsuit, Gable, she said, promised to provide her with a "$100,000 annuity" that, she claimed, he repeatedly told her over the years was set up in his will.

When, much to her chagrin, she discovered that no such

provision existed in the will, she filed a claim. It was rejected for lack of proof.

Gable did get the son he wanted: John Clark Gable grew up, married, and in 1989 starred in a little-seen western, *Bad Jim*. He looks a good deal like his father.

Judy Garland

HOLLYWOOD'S FAVORITE LITTLE GIRL—
next to Shirley Temple—earned, by some estimates, more than
$10 million in an entertainment career that spanned four
decades. But when Judy Garland finally succeeded in killing
herself, at the relatively young age of forty-seven, she died
broke.

Born Frances Ethel Gumm on June 10, 1922, to a theater
family in Grand Rapids, Michigan, Judy Garland was raised
in the entertainment business and never knew what anyone
would call a normal family existence until the last months of
her life. The star of the 1939 classic *The Wizard of Oz* once
described her own mother as "the real Wicked Witch of the
West," and Mama was not the only one to exploit her daughter's immense talent and good nature. During most of her
career, Garland allowed herself to be manipulated by those
who either wanted to live out their fantasies through her or else

line their pockets with the proceeds of her efforts. She would, for instance, not bother to read contracts before signing them. When she was out in public and fans would paw her, even grab at her, she'd wait for someone else, an agent or one of her five husbands, to intervene and protect her. This little girl naiveté and helplessness, coupled with her extraordinary gifts, endeared her to large audiences, but it also attracted to her the kind of men who wanted to take care of her—and take advantage.

Garland relied on pills early on in her film career: speed in the morning to get her going, and barbiturates at night to slow her down, and became hopelessly addicted. Her tolerance, especially for the sedatives, grew until the only way she could put herself to sleep was to overdose. She would awake in the middle of the night, forget how many pills she had downed, then pop some more. Once she was pronounced dead in a Hong Kong hospital after a massive overdose of Seconal; she took it during a screaming typhoon that had scared her quite literally out of her wits. Much of her trauma dated back to childhood and her hysterical, obsessive mother.

Where did all of Judy Garland's money go? Down the drain, most of it. According to her last husband, a New York club manager named Michael DeVinko (who went by the name Mickey Deans), Garland's mother frittered away her early earnings. After that the star was "managed" by various agents until she married her third husband, Sid Luft, with whom she had two children (Joey and Lorna). It was he who produced her successful 1954 comeback film, *A Star Is Born*.

Everybody took a cut of Judy Garland and Garland paid all the bills. Although she granted other people authority to run her life and probably never saw the stubs part of her checkbook, it undoubtedly was filled with the names of talent agents, press agents, managers, lawyers, and accountants. After their commissions came the fun stubs—liquor bills, traveling expenses, parties. And, after the fun diminished, the doctor and hospital bills. Whatever money remained was needed to keep her afloat through the long periods when she could not work because she was too impaired by her drug habit. (Apparently she drank very little.)

One entry that was missing from her checkbook was to the IRS. At one point she earned as much as $30,000 a week, but somebody in her entourage neglected to put aside anything for taxes. By the time she died, the Government had a bulging file on Judy Garland and she was in hock to the Treasury Department for about $500,000, a bill that was eventually paid off when her daughter Liza Minnelli embarked on a concert tour to raise money for that very purpose.

DeVinko/Deans, who married Garland just a few months before her death, estimated she was $1 million in the hole altogether. He had wanted to help her out, he said, by reclaiming a couple of rings she had pawned. Only he changed his mind when he learned that any jewelry she owned might be seized by the IRS to help clean up her tax bill. "That's why I can laugh at people who said I married her for the money," he told reporters.

DeVinko/Deans, thirty-five at the time, was one of those men who wanted to protect Garland. They were married and living in London at the start of 1969. Garland had performed especially badly at a London club after having shown up late, unprepared, and her voice in tatters. According to one account, some members of the audience actually booed and threw things at her. This was right on the heels of her having signed a terrible contract for a Scandinavian tour. As it was, she ended up sabotaging that engagement with drugs, causing her to lose her $10,000 advance.

In bad shape physically, gaunt and looking worn out, Garland nevertheless claimed she'd never been happier. DeVinko would later state that they spent their time together decorating their new home, learning to live as "Mr. and Mrs. Just Plain Folks" without servants and sycophants. He thought he was helping Garland cut back on the pills.

Then came the final straw: the sinking of a business deal that DeVinko had been trying to cement to put Garland's name on a chain of movie theaters. The backers of this project must have sensed disaster—to take one look at Garland was to see that she was teetering on the brink of death—and ultimately decided at the last minute not to use her name. DeVinko would later say that the deal would have set up Garland for life. Instead, the rug was pulled out from under her. By all accounts, she had run out of options—except the final one.

Four days after the theater deal collapsed, on a Sunday morning, the telephone awakened DeVinko in the cottage he and Garland shared in the swank London neighborhood of Belgravia. Friends were calling for Garland. But she wasn't in the bed where DeVinko had last seen her when he drifted off to sleep. Calling out her name, he got no answer. He tried the bathroom, but Garland had always locked the door, ever since she was a child actress using backstage toilets and could not find privacy any other way.

DeVinko found a bathroom window, it isn't clear how, and saw Garland sitting with her head slumped. When he broke in and lifted her head, blood oozed out of her mouth and nose. The coroner called it an accidental overdose.

Judy Garland wrote a couple of wills, the main one in

1961 at a low point in her career, when she was terminating her marriage to Sid Luft, and had adopted as her new caretakers two eager agent/promoters, David Begelman and Freddie Fields.

(She sued them in 1967 for mismanagement, but then dropped the suit and resumed doing business with them. The two men went on to found Creative Management Associates, a hugely successful Hollywood talent agency. Later Fields would become a Hollywood producer, while Begelman went on to become president of Columbia Pictures where he would be caught embezzling expense money.)

Garland's will, which was signed June 30, 1961, names Begelman and Fields as trustees of her estate, in charge of managing it in trust for her three children. (In addition to the two Luft offspring, Garland had a daughter, Liza, by her second husband, director Vincente Minnelli.)

The children were to receive income divided equally among them until they reached age twenty-one, and then they were to receive payments of principal, $250,000 each, when they turned twenty-five and thirty years of age. Any balances were to be paid out when they reached age thirty-five. But it was all tragically moot. The most anyone could find in assets came only to about $40,000, to apply against bills of about $1 million.

DeVinko claimed he and Garland had each signed wills leaving their estates to each other when they married. If true, he never exercised his rights or challenged her will. Perhaps he would still have been so noble if the theater deal had gone through, but he told reporters he was interested only in "helping Judy's children." In fact, DeVinko more or less disappeared off the face of the earth after Garland's ashes were buried in a Ferncliff Cemetary vault in Westchester County,

paid for by Liza. The remains sat for a year, awaiting intern-
ment, until the daughter could cover the cemetary's bill for
$37,500.

Lawyers for the estate did not bother trying to probate the
will until a full nine years after Garland's death, in 1978, after
Joey Luft reached twenty-one and enough time had passed for
an accumulation of royalties from films and recordings. The
estate had finally reached solvency but DeVinko desired no
part of it. He repeatedly dodged the process server, until the
court finally made the old will official by default.

DeVinko's name surfaced once more after that, in 1980.
He was working for an entertainment promoter named Roy
Radin (who was later murdered after a soured business deal in
connection with the 1984 film *The Cotton Club*) when police
had to be called to Radin's Southampton, Long Island, mansion during a party to rescue DeVinko. He had overdosed on
drugs.

Rita Hayworth

THE LOVE GODDESS OF THE 1940S GAVE MIL-
lions of American GIs something to daydream about when
they weren't fighting World War II, and five husbands something to remember. But Rita Hayworth forgot to leave a will.
Don't take her to task for it, though. She suffered with Alz-
heimer's disease. For the last sixteen or so years of her life Rita
Hayworth was not, as wills usually say, of sound mind.

Hayworth's life was one of those completely sordid tales
of Hollywood. Born in Brooklyn, of parents who were dancers
in vaudeville, Hayworth, when she was about twelve or thirteen, was put to work on the stage dancing with her father. She
eventually became the family's meal ticket, a pattern which
would be repeated many times in her life. Her real name was
Margarita Cansino and she made her first ten films under the
name Rita Cansino, usually playing a Latin temptress, before
she adopted her mother's maiden name, Hayworth.

While onstage her father played Hayworth's dance partner; off stage, he was her first lover, in a relationship that seems to have left her romantic instincts forever benighted. Her mother, meanwhile, was an alcoholic.

Rita's first husband, former car salesman Edward Judson, had consciously "created" her wildly successful Love Goddess persona, was twenty-two years her senior and, when things got rough, threatened to disfigure her with acid if she deserted him. He told her he had married her as an investment, insisted she sleep with other men to advance her career and, in the end, cost Hayworth $350,000 to buy her way out of the marriage.

Her second husband, actor-writer-director Orson Welles, was by most accounts the love of her life and they had a daughter together, Rebecca. But Welles was off working most of the time, or else thinking about running for public office, or, increasingly as time went on, busy having affairs with other women. Hayworth got tired of waiting around for him and filed for divorce.

Next she had a fling with Prince Aly Khan, the playboy son of the spiritual leader of the Ismaili Moslems. The affair caused an international sensation, with Khan compelled to divorce his wife and marry Hayworth in 1949. Together they had a daughter, Yasmin, who—once Hayworth divorced again—became the subject of a heated custody battle, with Khan accusing Hayworth of child neglect. As a settlement from the divorce she received $1.5 million ($7.65 million in 1990 dollars).

There were two more marriages after that, to singer Dick Haymes and director James Hill. Both men were riding the coattails of her fame, which, after the marriage to Aly Khan and her temporary removal from Hollywood, was quickly dissipating.

She appeared in sixty-one films altogether, including *Cover Girl* with Gene Kelly in 1944, *Strawberry Blonde* with James Cagney, and *You'll Never Get Rich* with Fred Astaire. Astaire once called her his favorite dancing partner.

But her film career ended forever in the 1960s when she could no longer memorize her lines. Observers on the set thought either she was drunk, or at least suffering from the effects of too many years of drinking. During the 1970s she traveled around the world a good deal, appearing at Rita Hayworth film festivals, although her condition appeared to degenerate and she was very often confused, disoriented, and sometimes violent.

Her younger daughter, Princess Yasmin Khan, came to the rescue when Hayworth was in danger of being institutionalized. The doctors still blamed acute alcoholism. But when Yasmin obtained legal control of her mother in 1981 she had her properly diagnosed. Yasmin moved Hayworth into an apartment next to hers in the San Remo, a stately apartment house overlooking Central Park in New York, and kept her as comfortable as possible. By 1986, Hayworth could not so much as walk across the room without assistance. The disease had totally destroyed her memory, leaving her as helpless and terrified as a child.

Hayworth died in 1987 at the age of sixty-eight, three days after a Rita Hayworth Gala at the Waldorf-Astoria Hotel raised $1.3 million for the Alzheimer's Disease Society.

She left an estate valued at $310,000, most of it represented by her pension from the Screen Actors Guild. It remains unclear how it was divided up. But her first daughter, Rebecca, signed a document indicating she did not care who was appointed to administer the estate.

In all, Hayworth's was a sad existence. Orson Welles, the one man Hayworth seemed to respect and who was candidly self-aware about his own shortcomings in their relationship, once said of their time together, "If this was happiness, imagine what the rest of her life had been."

Lillian Hellman

LILLIAN HELLMAN WAS A BRILLIANT WRITER
with a knack for constructing elaborate plots that were logical,
dealt with important issues, and drove the audience eagerly and
unrelentingly through the action to the climax. For this she
was rewarded. She was the most famous female playwright of
the twentieth century.

She was also the primary lover and friend for three
decades of Dashiell Hammett, the screenwriter and creator of
such American detective classics as *The Thin Man* and *The
Maltese Falcon*. She was a liberal political activist who, along
with Hammett, became involved in the labor movement of the
1930s, the progressive movement of the 1940s, and was put out
of work by the communist witch hunts in the 1950s. She had
a voracious sexual appetite that she worked hard to satisfy, and
displayed a terrible temper that was her principal trademark.
The paths of her life intersected with the lives of a wide range

of international movers and shakers in the arts and politics. She wrote not one but three memoirs, all of which became best-sellers, generated considerable political controversy, and led to charges that she persistently lied about and embellished her past. Hellman, it seems, was astute at creating her own legend.

She left a will that was just as complex and rich in characters and plot as her life and work. But unlike the scripts she was so adept at constructing, her will left dangling a few crucial loose ends. The judge who had to tie them up observed quite bluntly, "While her literary works can be characterized as creative genius, her will cannot."

The main problem was what to do with the half of the royalties from her work that she did not give to her longtime friend and principal heir, Peter Feibleman. Feibleman, thirty years her junior, was one of Hellman's closest friends by the time she died. The two writers—Feibleman lived in Hollywood and Hellman divided her time between New York and Martha's Vineyard—were collaborating on a book about their mealtimes together called, appropriately enough, *Eating Together*.

Feibleman came into Hellman's life by design: He campaigned for her friendship until he quite simply won her over. He had known her in New Orleans when he was a child, and would later claim he softened her up with expensive dinners, although there was never any suggestion that they had a romance. Hellman's biographers have said she undertook no romantic involvements after 1964, when she was fifty-nine.

Hellman was married once, to the writer Arthur Kober, whom she left for Dashiell Hammett in 1930. She divorced Kober two years later, although they remained friends. She never remarried; although she became pregnant at least twice, she chose to abort and died childless. Whether she would have left her money to any children she might have produced is anybody's guess. Hellman had managed to alienate so many people during her lifetime with her self-righteous angers, unrelenting vitriol, and her uncontrollable tantrums that the outpouring of affection upon her death was something of a shock to those who knew her well. When she turned on her enemies, and sometimes her friends, she burned them to their very foundations. Those who knew her were accustomed to prefacing every remark about her with, "You know, she isn't a nice person."

Hellman was born June 20, 1905, in New Orleans, into an extended family of upper-middle-class Jews. Part of her family ran a boardinghouse, and that is where she spent much of her childhood. Her father alternately worked in New Orleans and in New York, where he had well-to-do in-laws, and she grew up with a foot in each of these colorful worlds.

Lillian got her writing start as a publicist in New York, and was reading plays for producers while working on her own attempts at drama. She submitted one of her plays to a producer as though it had been selected from a pile she'd been given to read and urged him to produce it. The producer loved the script; when he learned that Hellman had written it he agreed to put it into production immediately. It was called *The Children's Hour*.

Thus did Hellman break into the big time at age twenty-nine, during the early years of her affair with Hammett. She would later say that it was he who gave her the story for the play and she brought to it the dialogue, character development, and pacing. It was an unusual story line for the early 1930s, in that it dealt with two young women wrongly accused of being lesbians at a girls' boarding school, and it was banned in some cities. Hellman's themes generally had to do with the corrosive elements of greed, power, and dishonesty, and stressed loyalty and moral courage.

Although Hellman and Hammett both had romantic involvements with other people during their lifetimes, and Hammett was married to someone else, the two remained close friends, and Hellman supported Hammett in the last several decades of his life after a crippling case of writer's block dried up both his creative juices and his income. He lived his last three years with Hellman in her New York apartment, finally dying in 1961 after years of alcoholism and chain smoking.

Hammett, for all of the literary success early in his life, died owing $220,000 (nearly $925,000 in 1990 dollars), $40,000 of it to Hellman and the rest in back taxes to the U.S. Government which, to satisfy the debt, had seized the rights to his work. He had left his estate, as insolvent as it was, in four parts: one to Hellman and the other three parts to his two daughters. Hellman persuaded the girls to sign over to her their rights to their father's work for nothing and then with one of her lovers she turned around and bought them back from the Government for $5,000.

Almost immediately, Hammett's work began to pay off again, making so much money that Hellman not only got back the $40,000 she had spent supporting Hammett, but she became a rich woman. In fact, Hellman confided to a friend before she died that "a great deal of the money" she eventually left—an estate worth almost $4.5 million—came from Hammett's work. (She did earn a reported $1 million herself from a 1982 Broadway revival of her play *The Little Foxes*, starring Elizabeth Taylor.)

Hellman lived well during those last twenty years, but never offered a nickel of the earnings to either of Hammett's daughters. However, in her will, she did leave the rights to them, finally fulfilling Hammett's last wishes. By that time, however, the rights had been milked dry. She also gave $35,000 in cash to each of Hammett's two grandchildren.

Although Hammett's daughters claimed to harbor no resentment toward her—they said they considered her their father's wife—William Wright, who wrote a biography of Hellman, concluded that, "Everything about her acquisition of the Hammett rights smacks of a shrewd, deliberate, and not very principled business maneuver." Hellman was famous for being strange about money. She once ran a display ad in the local paper on Martha's Vineyard complaining about the telephone service and asking readers to send her checks to cover the $183.60 cost of the notice.

If Hellman was a money-grubber and if she stole her fortune from Hammett's heirs, she was liberal about spreading it around when she was no longer able to enjoy it. She gave her friend Feibleman "any ten items he may choose" from among her personal belongings, fifty percent of all royalties from her literary work, the right to use and occupy her home on Martha's Vineyard, where she died, the right to buy her New York apartment, and $100,000 in cash. In a letter she wrote to Feibleman a year before she died, she told him about her decision to make him her principal heir, and said she hoped that the income he would receive from the royalties, half of about $100,000 a year, would provide enough money to keep him from having to write for movies if he didn't want to.

"You know that I want you to go back to being a novelist, and this does not have anything to do with looking down on writing pictures, because I liked writing them [for producer Sam Goldwyn, among others] and I see nothing wrong with it," wrote Hellman. "My belief is that you will be a happier man writing what you want to write. I have tried after my death to make that possible for you, and I have worked hard to see that the sums have come out right. In other words, enough to live on, but not enough to be silly Hollywood."

She left something to a long list of people. Some of them were cash bequests of up to $25,000, plus objects such as a highboy chest from her New York apartment and "any photograph of me as he may choose." To Mike Nichols, the director-producer, she left a Toulouse-Lautrec poster, some Italian sconces, and any manuscripts of hers found in the New York apartment. To her very close friends, John Hersey, the author, and his wife Barbara, she left a Queen Anne–style table from the Martha's Vineyard house, a platinum flower diamond pin, and "any and all paintings or pictures."

She even designated who was to receive her VCR.

She left smaller sums to a long list of friends and to two employees, $3,000 each.

After all the bequests—including one leaving all her original manuscripts, notes, and other papers to the University of Texas, in Austin—Hellman left the rest of her estate in two charitable trusts. The Lillian Hellman Fund was to provide grants to "any person to assist him or her in engaging in writing in any field or upon any subject, or in scientific research, anywhere in the world, who, in the opinion of the fiduciaries of this trust, is deserving of help."

The other, the Dashiell Hammett Fund, is—in light of subsequent events in eastern Europe—a textbook example of the fleeting nature of political fads. The Hammett Fund was to make grants for the advancement of political, social, and economic equality, civil rights, and civil liberties. "I further request," Hellman wrote, "that the fiduciaries in making such selections shall be guided by the political, social and economic beliefs which, of course, were radical, of the late Dashiell

Hammett who was a believer in the doctrines of Karl Marx."
Sic transit gloria mundi?

The problem with Hellman's will was that, after leaving
Feibleman half of her royalties, for as long as he lived, it didn't
make clear if the other half was supposed to go to the two
charitable trusts she'd set up. It took several years to answer
this question—a judge finally ruled "yes"—as well as others.

Hellman, who died at the age of seventy-eight in July
1984, was buried under a large pine tree in a cemetery in
Chilmark, Martha's Vineyard. The turnout for the funeral,
which was supposed to be small, shocked Hellman's friends
and the island. Famous people flew in from all over the world,
including Warren Beatty, Norman Mailer, Mike Wallace,
Ruth Gordon, Carl Bernstein, Jules Feiffer, and William Sty-
ron. It seemed that, for all her vitriol, Hellman had managed
to forge long-lasting, solid friendships. "Anger was her es-
sence," John Hersey said. "It informed her art. . . . [T]his
voltage of Lillian's was immensely important and valuable to
our time. It electrified a mood of protest. The protest was that
of every great writer, 'Life ought to be better than this.' "

Ernest Hemingway

"Time is the thing we have least of."

—*Told to Lillian Ross*

ERNEST HEMINGWAY MADE NO BONES ABOUT his intention to become a great writer. In fact, the greatest. A bold statement, certainly, but he paid dearly to realize this purpose. The personal injuries alone that he sustained in his quest for experience would have killed a lesser member of the species.

As for his celebrated clean writing style (his 1926 novel *The Sun Also Rises* is a casebook example of purified prose), Hemingway started streamlining his verbiage early on by mimicking Sherwood Anderson and Gertrude Stein. Soon, however, he created his own style. Pure Hemingway—the writer most associated with Paris, Madrid, Pamplona, Havana, Key West, Idaho, even, it has been suggested, Kansas City, Upper Michigan, and Smyrna. Hemingway lived to bring these places to life, and when that gift left him, he chose to call it a day. Literally.

Apropos of his writing style, Ernest Hemingway's will was just as laconic. Dated September 17, 1955, by which time the strain of his craft was showing, it was one page long.

For most of his life, while creating an astonishing body of work, winning both the Pulitzer and Nobel Prizes, earning riches, and establishing a literary and personal legend in his own time, Ernest Hemingway was a suicide looking for a place to happen. He was born July 21, 1899. When he was only twenty-seven he wrote, "The real reason for not committing suicide is because you always know how swell life gets again after the hell is over."

Two years later, his father pulled a gun on himself, while horribly depressed over his diabetic condition.

By the time Ernest was sixty-two, he was suffering from injuries sustained in two plane wrecks, during an African safari some seven years before, and from a diseased liver that had tolerated all it could of his years of drinking. And it was becoming very clear to Ernest that his life was never going to be quite so swell again. He was being treated with electroshock therapy for his depression when, on July 1, 1961, at his home in the Sawtooth Mountains near Sun Valley, Idaho, he blew his brains out with a double-barreled shotgun.

He had been married four times, first to his childhood sweetheart, Hadley Richardson. Married in 1919, they divorced in 1926. The next year he wed Pauline Pfeiffer. That lasted until 1940. Then came the novelist Martha Gellhorn in the same year. Hemingway quickly grew displeased with her. She would not accompany him on his yacht, the *Pillar,* and accused *him* of holding back *her* literary career. (American lit wags joke five decades later: "When was the last time you read a book by Martha Gellhorn?") Finally, in 1944, came his fourth and final wife, Mary Welsh, a journalist. She was to receive just about everything, despite Hemingway's leaving several children.

"I have intentionally omitted to provide for my children now living or for any that may be born after this will has been executed as I repose complete confidence in my beloved wife Mary to provide for them according to written instructions I have given her. . . . In Witness Whereof, I have hereunto set my hand and seal to this my last Will and Testament at Finca Vigia San Fancisco de Paula—Cuba. Ernest Miller Hemingway."

The estate was valued at approximately $1.4 million ($5.88 million in 1990 dollars), and included property valued at $801,766.51 and stocks and bonds totaling $418,933.32. Literature paid off, for once. His personal art collection contained at least two valuable paintings: a Paul Klee titled *The Monument*, worth $9,000, and *The Farm* by Miró, assessed at $5,000. Hemingway died owing the Government about $50,000, and, for tax purposes, the total value of all the unexpired copyrights to his works was set at $179,000. (They ranged in individual worth from as little as $1,065 for *Winner Take Nothing* to, at the top of the list, $61,429 for *The Old Man and the Sea*, based on sales from the previous few years.)

Hemingway's publisher, Charles Scribner, personally wrote the IRS to estimate what his famous late author's books might be earning in the first five years after his death. Scribner painted a dark portrait.

"It is the normal experience of publishers to find that sales of a deceased author, even one of world renown, decline markedly in the years following his or her death," wrote Scribner. He cited as examples his own house's experience with James M. Barrie, Edith Wharton, John Galsworthy, and F. Scott Fitzgerald.

"In the case of Ernest Hemingway," continued Scribner, "it would be reasonable to suppose that the same pattern of declining sales would be followed and probably with a more pronounced decline insofar [as] while this author while alive contributed substantially to the sales of his works by the unusually widespread interest in the events of his life."

Scribner seemed to think that without the press to whet the public's interest in the latest exploits of Hemingway, the public would no longer be interested in buying his books. Scribner was wrong.

Jimi Hendrix

IF CRITICS THOUGHT HIS PERFORMANCES and musical output were chaotic—this chap played his guitar on his back, with his teeth, and occasionally smashed the instrument to bits against the amplifiers to end his act—they should have taken a look at the mess that '60s music-maker Jimi Hendrix left his heirs.

Hendrix left behind as his most famous piece of music a tortured rendition of "The Star-Spangled Banner," memorialized on film in the 1970 documentary of the 1969 rock concert at Woodstock, New York. Hendrix entered the business typically, learning the guitar by playing along with Muddy Waters records at home and then appearing in black clubs in Nashville and Harlem. In the early years he played backup guitar to such big-name stars as Little Richard, The Isley Brothers, and Joey Dee.

Failing to make it in this country, where he was born

James Marshall Hendrix in Seattle, he broke into the big-time in England where he formed his own group. With Mitch Mitchell on drums and Noel Redding on bass, he called it the Jimi Hendrix Experience, and recorded a hit song, *Hey Joe*. Jimi wrote many of his own numbers, and his signature dynamic, hip-swiveling performance drove teenaged audiences crazy. One appearance, at the Singer Bowl on Long Island in 1967, made headlines for the pandemonium it created. By then, Hendrix was already a big, best-selling star, with tunes such as *Purple Haze* and *Foxy Lady,* and he could command as much as $50,000 per performance. The haze he referred to, of course, was created by drugs; it was drugs that did him in. Hendrix was almost always flying on something by the time he achieved stardom. In concert, he was known to lean over the edge of the stage, open his mouth, and accept unidentified pills from adoring fans.

This frequently failed to enhance his performances, and near the end of his rather short life he sometimes was unable to play. At one gig, in Madison Square Garden, he threw down his guitar and stalked off stage. His career was already shaky when downers finally got the better of him. The coda took place in London in 1970 with a groupie, an ex-girl friend of Mick Jagger's. Hendrix accidentally swallowed a few too many sleeping pills and vomited in his sleep, causing him to suffocate. He was twenty-seven years old.

Hendrix left an estate eventually valued at $2.6 million ($8.32 million in 1990 dollars) before debts of about $1 million, and a daughter he had fathered in 1966 when he was living in California with a sixteen-year-old girl named Diana Carpenter. Tamika Laurice James—Hendrix's original stage name had been Jimi James—was born in 1967 in Davenport, Iowa, Diana's hometown. A guardian representing Tamika claimed that Hendrix was scheduled to have blood tests taken in November 1970 (two months after Hendrix died) to establish paternity and set up support payments. The guardian, whose court filings reveal a unique approach to the English language and merely a nod to its spelling, complained that Hendrix's "failure to take the blood tests seem to be not an unusual part of the deceased's eratic [sic] behavior. His sense of responsibility was lost in the maze of his fame and his self-indulgence in stardom. His attitude of irresponsibility and benevolence [sic] toward my ward now condemns her to the medieval concept of a 'non-person.' " This was followed by a quote from Shakespeare, "Why bastard? wherefore base?"

In describing Hendrix's career, the guardian wrote the court that, "His rise to fame was velocious [sic]. In the few short years from 1966 to his death in 1970, [he] shot from the abyss of the unknown to an entertainer of stellar status."

A judge rejected Tamika's claim on the Hendrix estate, and the late musician's father, James, got it all. The senior Hendrix originally requested that his late son's lawyer Henry W. Steingarten be appointed administrator of the estate. Then he found out that Steingarten also represented Jimi Hendrix's agent, Michael Jeffrey, and had also done so during Hendrix's life. In one instance, James Hendrix claimed, Steingarten had paid Jeffrey $20,000, even though Jeffrey owed the estate $33,000 in royalty payments.

As such, the father accused the two men of collusion—and Steingarten of overcharging—and asked Steingarten to resign, which he did.

Harry Houdini

IF HEIRS ARE LUCKY, THEY ARE LEFT HAPPY
memories of the deceased as well as cash, art, jewelry, real
estate—items of tangible value. Harry Houdini left some of
these, but he also bequeathed an estate rich in intangibles—the
professional secrets of a master magician. In his will he ordered
them all destroyed.

Houdini was born Ehrich Weiss to Jewish parents in
Budapest, Hungary, on March 24, 1874. Shortly after his birth
the family moved to America, settling in Appleton, Wisconsin,
where Houdini's father became the local rabbi. Unfortunately,
however, the elder Weiss was unable to adapt to the new
world, and especially to the boondocks of Wisconsin. The
congregation unceremoniously fired him and the family moved
to New York, where his five surviving sons took up supporting
him and his wife. Houdini's first job in New York, at the age
of fourteen in 1888, was cutting linings for a necktie manufac-

turer. It was fortuitous employment: He and another boy at the factory, Jacob Hyman, shared an interest in magic, as well as sports and fitness, and began to learn tricks and appear together in amateur shows.

Houdini attended a séance once, and was amazed at how people could—in his eyes—be fooled into believing they had been contacted by ghosts of loved ones. He was especially fascinated by a trick used by spiritual mediums to prove their authenticity: letting themselves be tied up in a chair. The teenager discovered that the mediums would in fact escape during the darkness of the séance in order to ring bells and make creepy sounds they claimed were ghosts, only to return to their bonds before the lights were turned up. The two boys practiced tying each other up, and learned that the more elaborate the rope effects, the easier it could be to escape.

Then, at the age of seventeen, the rabbi's son read the memoirs of Jean-Eugène Robert-Houdin, a Parisian magician who was once called upon by the Government of France to dazzle a tribe of rebellious and superstitious Algerian nomads into peaceful submission. Ehrich Weiss became convinced that magic was the career for him. He and Jacob established themselves as a team, taking their stage name from Houdin's, adding an "i" at the end, and calling themselves the Houdini Brothers. But Jacob lacked Erich's fire in the belly. After only four months, the act broke up. Houdini then took a new partner, his brother, Theo.

Harry, as he now called himself, met his one and only wife, Wilhelmina Beatrice ("Bess") Rahmer, in 1894, when they were booked into Coney Island. He was twenty, and she was eighteen and part of a sister song-and-dance team. Within two weeks they were married and Houdini had replaced Theo in his act—with Bess.

For the next thirty years Houdini refined his craft, learning ever more dangerous stunts, and zealously debunking the claims of mystics, mediums, and psychics. Spiritualism was a huge fad at the time and Houdini assumed the role of consumer-advocate, keeping an eagle eye on the magic racket. He challenged every mystic and medium to prove their "acts," especially when they summoned the dead. None could; and Houdini was responsible for sending a few to jail on charges of fraud.

His obsession with truth-in-mysticism was actually based on his desire to find and then communicate with a true spirit world. The great love of Houdini's life was his mother, and one of his major preoccupations was death, especially hers. He lived in terror of the day she would die, spending three decades trying to ensure that he would be able to speak to her in the afterlife. He never did. When, finally, his mother did die, at the age of seventy-two, Houdini fainted on the spot.

He was similarly obsessed with his own death. Apparently he had some inkling that the end was near when, in 1926, he had made for one of his stunts an expensive, elaborate bronze coffin. The trick itself was an underwater submersion in a sealed box for ninety minutes.

At the beginning of October of that year Bess contracted a serious case of food poisoning. Houdini himself was experiencing severe insomnia, but her illness kept him awake nearly 'round the clock. Once it was clear Bess was free from danger, Houdini made a quick business trip to New York from Albany, where his act had been playing. After three sleepless nights of travel and worry about Bess, he broke an ankle bone during one of his stunts. The pain was severe and he lost even more sleep. Still, he fashioned a leg brace of his own device and the show went on.

A week later the show moved to Montreal. After lecturing on spiritualist fraud at McGill University, Houdini allowed a young artist to come backstage and sketch him. During the session, another student showed up to return a book he had borrowed from Houdini. The student began questioning the magician, asking if it was true that he could take a direct blow to the stomach. (Houdini remained an avid physical-fitness nut his entire life.) Houdini admitted that he could, assuming that he knew the blow was coming and could prepare for it. To test the magician's claim, without warning the student punched Houdini in the gut as hard as he could. As Houdini doubled over in pain, the student struck him three more times, before the artist and a third student could subdue him.

That evening, Houdini did his performance, thinking the pain in both his stomach and ankle was muscular and would clear up with time. When the show packed up, the pain was intensified. In Detroit a nurse took his temperature: 102 degrees. A doctor told Houdini that his appendix had been ruptured, and he would have to go to the hospital immediately. But Houdini refused. Once again the show went on. Finally, after delaying even further, he checked into the hospital.

Houdini's appendix was removed, but the infection, which had been circulating and poisoning his bloodstream for three days, had caused irreversible damage. He hung on for another week. But he realized the end was near. He held Bess's hand to his heart and told her that, if it were possible, he would speak to her from the spirit world. He instructed her that the secret code he would use would be: *"Rosabelle,"* followed by *"Believe."* He died on October 31, Halloween.

He was buried in his bronze coffin next to his mother in a New York cemetery, his head resting on a black bag stuffed with the letters she had written to him through his life.

His will was fairly complicated. He left his dramatic library, all household effects, furniture, trophies, silverware, ornaments, jewelry, diamonds, and personal effects "including my oil paintings" to his wife.

The rest of his library and "collection of programmes" he donated to the Library of Congress. To the American Society of Psychical Research he originally left "my collection of books, pamphlets, letters, and the like relating to spiritualism, occultism, and psychical research absolutely and forever." But, having second thoughts about that, he drew up a codicil, changing the beneficiary to the Library of Congress. Even in death Houdini was a skeptic.

The most interesting bequest was the one leaving "all my lithographs, theatrical effects, new mysteries, and illusions and accompanying paraphernalia" to his brother, Theo, with whom he had performed as a young man. The will stated that all of this material was, upon Theo's death, to be "burnt and destroyed."

Theo was also to give $50 (approximately $365 in 1990 dollars) each year to his nephew (Theo's son) for a period of twenty years on June 16th, which was the birthdate of their mother. It was Harry's way of keeping her memory alive.

He left $500 ($3,650 in 1990 dollars) each to several of his longtime assistants. Then he divided up the balance of the estate equally among Bess and his five siblings, Nathan, Theo, Leopold, William, and his sister Carrie. Although Harry married a Catholic and left no children, he insisted that, in order for Theo to receive his share of the estate, he must have his children "confirmed according to Jewish law and traditions" within three months of Harry's death.

Airing some dirty laundry, Harry also specified that Leo's inheritance could not in any way benefit his wife. She had originally been Nathan's wife, but left him for brother Leo, outraging the family, especially the mother. Houdini was ready to forgive Leopold for wife-swapping, but was waiting for his mother to issue her forgiveness first from the other side. She never did, so Leo remained ostracized and his share presumably was never spent on his wife.

As for Bess's contacting Harry after he died, numerous mediums attempted to act on her behalf. One claimed to have been successful and even came up with the secret code— *"Rosabelle . . . believe."*

At first Bess thought it was the real thing. But then she later remembered having confided the code to a friend. Bess never spoke to her husband again.

Gypsy Rose Lee

AS THE MOST FAMOUS FEMALE TO SHUCK off her clothes since Lady Godiva, Gypsy Rose Lee deserves her niche as one of the versatile women of the twentieth century and certainly one of the earliest proponents of the modern Women's Lib movement. She was an ecdysiast—in everyday parlance, a stripper—but she was never cheap or vulgar, and she raised the level of what she did to an art.

As a matter of fact, so refined, and celebrated, was this queen of burlesque that in 1940 Rodgers and Hart were inspired to base a song in their musical show *Pal Joey* upon her. Called "Zip," the number identified "Miss Lee" by name and detailed her intellectual curiosity—as she stripped.

When not shedding her clothes Lee was often writing, though it wasn't until she hung up her boa for good in 1956, and sat down to write her memoirs, that Gypsy created her most lasting legacy. Published the following year, her autobiography *Gypsy* was adapted into the 1959 Broadway stage smash starring Ethel Merman (and subsequent 1962 movie version with Rosalind Russell). Its tale of the desperately determined stage mother who forces her insecure daughter into show business exists as a pinnacle of musical-stage achievement, and is likely to be playing somewhere in the world for as long as there are mothers and daughters and stages on which to perform.

Gypsy could not claim a daughter of her own, but she did produce an only son named Erik, born in 1944, and it was he—as confidante, dresser, prop man, and stagehand, all before he turned twelve—who helped run her rather chaotic existence and who inherited all she had collected during her lengthy and colorful career.

Born Rose Louise Hovick (she signed both names on her will) in Seattle on February 9, 1914, Gypsy Rose Lee made her stage debut when she was four, then later appeared on the vaudeville circuit with her sister June Havoc. They called themselves "Madame Rose's Dancing Daughters." With vaudeville dying all around them, thanks to the growing popularity of radio, Louise got herself a gimmick—she stripped like a lady. The gimmick quickly paid off.

Having made a name for herself, she was also able to break into publishing circles. She authored two mystery novels, one of which, *The G-String Murders,* was turned into the 1943 film *The Lady of Burlesque*; the other, *The Naked Genius,* was a best-seller. A play of hers also served as the basis for the screenplay of the 1946 movie *Doll Face.*

Except it was as a stripper that the public recognized Gypsy, and she was shrewd enough to play the reputation for all it was worth. Once she retired the G-string and started telling people, "Oh honey, I haven't taken off my clothes for years," she took to worrying about what she would do for money. The book and show *Gypsy* solved that problem, although she was never certain how long that source of income would last. So she developed a one-woman show about her life, and took it on the road—in her 1956 four-door Rolls-Royce sedan. In the end, she made more money telling the story of being a stripper than she ever made being one.

Besides having affairs with heavyweight New York producers Billy Rose (who was once married to Fanny Brice), and Michael Todd (who married Elizabeth Taylor, among others), Lee was married three times. She had Erik when she was wed to the antiques dealer William Kirkland. But, as Erik was to discover one day when Kirkland refused to continue paying for Erik's psychiatrist, Erik was not his father's son. It took some prodding, but Lee finally confessed that she had instigated an affair with the Viennese-born Hollywood filmmaker Otto Preminger specifically to become pregnant by him.

Why did she choose Preminger, considered a brute until his dying day, when she knew Billy Rose, reputedly one of the richest men in America, or Mike Todd, considered one of the most exciting and certainly the most flamboyant? Quite simply, besides the fact that she thought Todd "had a mean streak" which she feared a child might inherit, she found Preminger to be the most genetically suitable man available at the time. Once Lee did become pregnant, she brushed off Preminger and raised the boy alone.

The revelation nearly destroyed what had previously been a warm, close mother-son relationship. As she lay dying years later, Lee said of Preminger: "I sensed he was a good man, in spite of his reputation. That's one of the reasons I picked him. That and his mind." She sought to have a child by him, she said, because, "I felt so alone that I decided to have something no one would ever be able to take away from me."

No one did. Her will was signed November 15, 1969, and she was dead from lung cancer on April 26 the next year. Everything went to Erik; anyone else who wished to stake any sort of claim was to receive one dollar. Her estate was valued at $575,000 ($1.84 million in 1990 dollars), which in addition to her stocks and bonds included $271,000 in cash. She had sold her rights to *Gypsy* for a lump sum, sometime around the end of the first run of the show, in the early '60s. The Rolls was sold for $8,250, its current value at the time, and with it went a 1959 Fiat Convertible Sedan, for $220. Her clothing and other belongings were auctioned off by Sotheby Parke-Barnet and fetched $21,000.

Her huge inventory of art was appraised at more than $80,000. Her taste, not surprisingly, was quite eclectic. Besides a small, unsigned Picasso ink drawing of wrestlers, worth $2,750 in 1970, she had collected a Chagall town scene oil valued at $50,000; a Georgia O'Keeffe pastel titled "Lillies," worth $2,000; a Cocteau drawing worth $300, and seven Fanny Brice ink still life paintings, worth, *in toto,* $200. In addition, she had an extensive collection, fourteen works in all, of Julio de Diego's. He was her third husband.

As for Erik, with his mother's permission before she died he contacted Preminger, and the two men began a warm friendship. A year after Gypsy's death, Preminger legally adopted Erik, who officially changed his surname from Kirkland to Preminger. The two men even shared a singular professional collaboration, when Erik wrote the screenplay for his father's 1975 film *Rosebud,* although it was a flop. By the mid-1980s, Erik Lee Preminger was a San Francisco–based TV reporter, covering the arts and interviewing celebrities—although rarely as fascinating as the one he grew up with.

John Lennon

JOHN WINSTON ONO LENNON LIVED HIS LIFE in just about the most public manner possible. He even died that way, gunned down by a demented fan at the doorway to his apartment building. Lennon's career may have demanded a public life, but he overstepped the boundaries of a simple entertainment career, putting on such stunts as the famous "lie-in" in Montreal where he and wife Yoko Ono recorded "Give Peace a Chance." And he participated with her in numerous public protests ranging from antiwar rallies to support of an artist jailed in the Midwest for possession of two marijuana cigarettes. He and Yoko portrayed themselves to the world as simple, peace-loving music- and merry-makers who wanted the world to share the enlightened wholesomeness of their lives and their efforts to make the planet á better place to live.

So much for the public Lennon. There were a few things about which the ex-Beatle was fiercely private. One of them was certainly money. Whether this was an expression of guilt or embarrassment about his wealth, or perhaps a feeling that the "radical" politics of such a rich man might earn him the label of limousine liberal, or whether he was simply trying to discourage fund-raisers and kidnappers, Lennon eschewed talk about money while he was alive, and his last will is nearly silent on the subject. In fact, it was structured in such a way that outsiders would not be able to figure out how much he was really worth, or even how exactly it was to be spread around once he was gone.

In court papers filed after his death, Lennon's estate was estimated by one attorney to be valued in excess of $30 million ($50 million in 1990 dollars). But in his 1984 biography of Lennon, writer Ray Coleman put the figure at closer to $150 million, and growing at the rate of $50,000 a day in royalties from his songs and recordings. Whatever the total, it was a fortune; and it can be properly deduced roughly what part of it went to Yoko.

For all that drugs, booze, sex, and violence typically season a rock-and-roll career, Lennon was a family man at heart. He married young, at twenty-one, to one of his college girl friends, Cynthia Powell, who bore him the first of his two sons, Julian Lennon, later to become a performer himself. They divorced in 1968, after Lennon had started dating Yoko Ono.

Cynthia Powell (she later remarried a couple of times, eventually becoming Cynthia Twist) has said that Lennon was an insanely jealous husband and, strangely, demanded reassurances even as their marriage was ending that she had always been faithful to him. Meanwhile, Lennon had been merrily cheating on her with Ono and demanding to know all the details of *her* past sex life. Apparently Lennon could be quite a chauvinist.

When it came time to settle for the divorce with Cynthia, Lennon paid her off with £100,000 (roughly $530,000 in 1990 U.S. dollars) and promised to make a "generous and proper provision for Julian," including money for school fees. The trust that Lennon set up for Julian was to provide him £100,000 at the age of twenty-five. The boy was to be the only beneficiary of the will unless Lennon fathered other children. When Yoko gave birth to their only child, Sean, in 1975, the trust was split in half and each of the youngsters was to receive £50,000.

Eleven years after the divorce from Cynthia, on November 12, 1979, in an office he maintained in his apartment in the landmark Dakota apartment building overlooking Central Park, Lennon signed his last will. Present were his attorney, David Warmflash, three witnesses, and probably Ono as well. The three witnesses signed a short statement that said, in part, that they were fairly certain that Lennon "could read, write, and converse in the English language and was suffering from no defect of sight, hearing or speech, or from any other physical or mental impairment which would affect his capacity to make a valid Last Will and Testament."

The will itself was skimpy, just four typewritten, double-spaced pages, including the signature page:

"Should my wife survive me, I give . . . an amount equal to that portion of my residuary estate, the numerator and denominator of which shall be determined as follows:

"1. The numerator shall be an amount equal to one-half (½) of my adjusted gross estate less the value of all other property included in my gross estate . . . [that will have] passed to my wife either under any other provision of this Will or in any manner outside of this Will in such manner as to qualify for and be allowed as a marital deduction [for the purposes of inheritance taxes]. . . .

"2. The denominator shall be an amount representing the value of my residuary estate [what would be left over after bequests, expenses and taxes]."

In other words, Ono, whom Lennon referred to in the will as "my beloved wife" and often called "mother," was to inherit roughly half of the estate. The other half, or whatever remained, was to be added to the existing trust of which Julian and Sean were presumably major beneficiaries. There is a hint in the court papers that Lennon may have left something for Cynthia too.

Also, according to a biographer, "many of the beneficiaries would have been charities." Lennon and Ono had set up Spirit Foundation as the philanthropic arm of their lives, and automatically ten percent of their income was tithed to it. Spirit was in the business of dispensing money to a wide range of worthy causes, from senior citizens' homes to handicapped children. In the years immediately after Lennon's death, Ono sold off some of the properties they had acquired together, and was reportedly going to give about £3 million (about $5 million U.S.) to various charities around the world.

The trust referred to in Lennon's will was to be distributed "in accordance with the terms of that [trust] agreement and any amendments made pursuant to its terms before my death." By this time his sons' inheritances must have been enhanced to much more than the £50,000 apiece they were promised in 1968.

According to a lawyer representing the interests of Sean, who was five years old when Lennon was murdered, the estate was deliberately tied up in other trust agreements that did not have to be filed with the courts. Lennon's "property was disposed of in this manner because he believed strongly that it was a private and family matter which should be kept that way," attorney Paul J. Powers said in court papers. "I was permitted to examine the trust agreement [on Sean's behalf]." In fact, presumably to exert full legal authority, Powers—and not the boy's mother—was made Sean's guardian.

Powers said further that Sean was getting less than the one-third of Lennon's estate (not counting the trust fund) that he would have gotten if there had been no will at all. The other two-thirds would have gone to Ono and Julian Lennon. But, Powers added, "Without going into detail as to its provisions, it is sufficient to say that it makes provision for my ward as to income and principal which, under all circumstances, are not unreasonable."

The last provision of Lennon's will disinherited anyone who tried to contest it: Any of the beneficiaries or trustees who tried to "institute or prosecute or be in any way interested or instrumental in the institution or prosecution of any action or proceeding for the purpose of setting aside or invalidating this Will, then and in each such case, I direct that such legatee or beneficiary shall receive nothing whatsoever under this Will or the . . . trust."

On the evening of December 8, 1980, nearly a year and a month to the day after the will was signed, and in the doorway of the very same building, one of Lennon's fans, Mark David Chapman, stepped out of the shadows by a side entrance as Lennon and Ono returned home from a recording session.

"Mr. Lennon?" Chapman called out. As Lennon turned to respond, Chapman pumped five rounds from a .38 caliber revolver into his back. Lennon died that night from a massive loss of blood.

A year earlier Lennon and Ono had donated $1,000 to the New York City Police Department. The purpose of their gift was to buy the officers some bulletproof vests.

Alan Jay Lerner

THE EXTRAORDINARILY GIFTED MAN COULD write poetry to music but he couldn't write a simple check to the IRS. As a result, Alan Jay Lerner's heirs faced the nightmare that ordinary people usually joke about—a potentially lucrative estate buried under a mountain of debt, in the form of a nearly $3 million bill for unpaid income taxes. The world-class American lyricist had moved to England in the last years of his life, and stopped paying U.S. income taxes. One of the reasons he stayed abroad, according to his attorney, "was partly the result of the fact that he owed a great deal of money to the IRS." The government claimed he owed taxes as far back as 1975, nine years before he died.

Lerner made a treasury full of money in his career as a playwright and lyricist. In collaboration with the composer Frederick Loewe, Lerner's most towering achievements are

My Fair Lady, the film musical *Gigi,* and *Camelot.* Record sales for his 1956 stage phenomenon *My Fair Lady* alone totaled $19 million ($95 million in 1990 dollars), and it remains a hallmark among Broadway scores. Their first theater hit together was in 1947, *Brigadoon,* a fairy tale about a Scottish town that comes to life for one day every 100 years. Among its popular songs are "Almost Like Being in Love." Lerner won three Academy Awards in his lifetime, including one for *Gigi,* which in 1959 won nine Academy Awards altogether.

But as someone who wrote about the good life in his works, Lerner was also accustomed to living it. He was born wealthy (the family owned a chain of dress shops bearing its name) and he was known as a party boy; at one point in his career he owned both a Manhattan townhouse with eight bathrooms and a vacation villa on the Riviera.

He also displayed an expensive habit in women. He was married eight times, predictably requiring seven expensive divorce settlements. In his 1978 autobiography, *The Street Where I Live,* he observed, "I had no flair for marriage. I also had no flair for bachelorhood. Marriage, as someone once said, is often like a besieged fortress. Everyone inside wants to get out and everyone outside wants to get in."

His last wife, Liz Robertson, was an English musical comedy actress with whom he lived in London. They met when she was about to star as Eliza Doolittle in a revival of *My Fair Lady,* and it was with Robertson that Lerner flew to New York for cancer treatments, and it was there that Lerner died in 1986 of lung cancer. He was sixty-seven, and had been a compulsive nail-biter—and smoker.

Whether he was crying poor for the benefit of the IRS,

or whether he really was strapped for cash, Lerner's lawyer and executor of his estate claimed in court papers, after the death, that the only articles the lyricist had owned in New York were ninety boxes of personal property that he failed to have sent to England because "the cost was immense and Mr. Lerner was waiting for a propitious time when there would be funds available or when he would be able to arrange a less expensive method of shipment."

For Lerner, the party was over. Still, in his will he left $1,000 to two friends, Benjamin Welles of *The New York Times,* and Sidney Gruson, *Times* chairman. The will stated, "The purpose of this modest remembrance is to defray the cost of one evening's merriment to be devoted to cheerful recollections of their departed friend." The *Times* men organized a superstar memorial to Lerner in a Broadway theater, at which Lerner's original Eliza, Julie Andrews, affectionately sang his favorite song, "If Love Were All," by Noël Coward.

Lerner left something "to my devoted secretary, Judy Insel," all of his personal property and real estate to his wife, and the rest of his estate—the most valuable asset of which were the copyrights to his work—in trust, with the majority of the income to be divided up among his wife, his children, and his grandchildren on a percentage basis: ten percent each to two granddaughters; five percent each to two daughters; ten percent to his son; and 55 percent to his wife, which was to be paid to her only during her lifetime. After that, her share was to be divided up among his offspring and their children. The will pointed out that the reason his daughters received a lower percentage than his son was, "not . . . a difference in love and affection but is because I made a special settlement to [their] mother at the time of our divorce."

Lerner said he wanted to be cremated, and directed that "there be no funeral and no religious ceremony of any kind in connection with my death. If God does not know me by now, no words by a stranger will help to introduce me."

Elsa Maxwell

IF ELSA MAXWELL WERE ALIVE AND ACTIVE
today, she might be called a club promoter. But contemporary
she was not. Besides, she would have looked awful in Spandex.

Elsa Maxwell's heyday began after World War I, at a
time when this country initially matured as a world power;
when she died in 1962 the press remembered her as "the best
known party-giver in America and maybe in the world." Like
the celebrated parties she gave, however, when her glittering
life was over there was not much left beyond the memories, the
echo of the music and laughter, and the trash to be taken out.

Her will left little of tangible value, except for some
well-worn party accessories.

She was born in 1883 in Keokuk, Iowa, and grew up in
San Francisco, where her father was a newspaper columnist.
Brash and perky, she was bitten by the society bug when her
family was snubbed for a party invitation by some rich swells.

Turning that rejection into a lifelong passion to be at the center of society, she ended up pulling it off with a vengeance.

During Maxwell's life she managed to rub shoulders with, and throw parties for, anyone who was anybody in the arts, science, and society on two continents, including Freud, Einstein, Caruso, Eisenhower, Churchill, Gershwin, Noël Coward, Fanny Brice, the Duke and Duchess of Windsor, George Bernard Shaw, and Cole Porter, to name but a few of her nearest and dearest.

Maxwell became famous herself by ingratiating herself with the rich and renowned and showing them a rousing good time. She experienced a brief career in theater as a vaudeville actress and piano accompanist, becoming known as a good girl to have around at a party even though she possessed the figure and face of a bulldog. That hardly mattered. Knowing how to put on a good show, she became popular with wealthy society in New York and in the capitals of Europe. At one of the parties she sponsored, the fish course was announced by releasing live seals in the ballroom.

She once explained her success this way: "Most rich people are the poorest people I know. Guilt complexes stemming from the way they made, married, or inherited their money warp their normal outlets of warmth and vitality. I brought to them a capacity for friendship and gaiety that offered escape from plush-bottomed boredom, casual sex without passion, and excessive gambling without excitement. I have been called a parasite for accepting the largesse of the wealthy, but I contributed as much, at least, as I received. I had imagination and they had money, a fair exchange of the commodity possessed by each side in greatest abundance."

In addition to playing the piano and acting, she was a partner in two Paris nightclubs, consultant to a dressmaker, and press agent for Monte Carlo, helping to put that European playground on the map. Later she wrote a newspaper society column and a couple of books, though her income from these endeavors was hardly enough to support her in grand style, if any style at all. Most of the bills for her lavish living expenses were picked up for her by the restaurants or hotels she supplied with reams of publicity, or else by the rich people for whom she staged the extravagant soirées.

Admirers were constantly giving her things. A French couturier insisted on gifting her with fourteen of his original creations each year, because he knew she'd wear them and gain him some notoriety, even though she was old at the time and as dumpy as she had ever been. A prosperous newspaper publisher once gave her a $5,000 credit at Cartier in Paris for her birthday; she persuaded the benefactor to let her use the money instead to hire the famous violinist, Fritz Kreisler, to play for one of her parties.

She denied frequent charges that she took fees for the parties, or blackmailed people to suppress scandals about them, or collected kickbacks from caterers. She claimed that the only direct cash aid she received was from a few close, rich friends, and that it never amounted to much more than $20,000 during her entire lifetime. The Waldorf-Astoria in New York at one point provided her with a free suite, because she attracted so much business. Maxim's, the four-star Paris restaurant, always "lost" the bill when she showed up, because she brought with her a crowd of well-heeled patrons and plenty of attendant publicity.

In 1954 she published her memoirs, in which she went on at length about the evils of idle wealth. She complained about the "what's-in-it-for-me? attitude that permeates the upper crust on the continent today," and proclaimed that England "was the only country that was not disgraced by its upper class."

When she died of heart failure in 1963 at age eighty, it was only a week after attending her last party, the annual April in Paris ball, an event she instigated in the early 1950s. She had been active right up to the end.

Maxwell never married, never had children, and may never have had a beau. She professed to have been attracted to three men in her life, but if these romantic feelings were consummated she never said.

Her only beneficiary was an old chum, Dorothy Fellowes-Gordon, whom she had known for more than fifty years, and who had been her constant companion in the last three years of her life. Fellowes-Gordon tried to track down relatives, but could not.

Maxwell left her everything to "Dickie" in a terse, businesslike, twenty-eight-line will. "Everything" included $1,200 in French francs and $7,600 in a bank account. Maxwell also had $15.74 in walking-around money. Her personal belongings and jewelry added up to a value of $2,190, including a worn-out mink coat worth $225; a "badly worn" white fox scarf valued at $35; "thirty odd pieces of luggage, very poor condition," set at $50; and a "gold bridge for teeth" appraised at $8. She died owing the Summit Hotel in New York where she lived $662.97 (she had by then departed from the Waldorf); $91.93 to Saks Fifth Avenue; $11.73 to Elizabeth Arden; and $300 to a furrier at the Waldorf. All told, her estate added up to $12,146.17 (nearly $50,000 in 1990 dollars).

In a respectful *New York Times* interview five months before she died, Maxwell explained, "I have no money to speak of, and no more possessions than I can carry with me. But I have more friends than any living person. They are my riches."

Margaret Mead

WHEN SHE GAVE BIRTH TO HER CHILD, anthropologist Margaret Mead insisted on having the delivery filmed. Having heard that a child's temperament can be read in its face at birth, she wanted to study the film for clues on how best to know and raise the child. She even held up her labor for ten minutes so the friend who was operating the camera and lights could run out to the car to replace a burned-out bulb.

Margaret Mead studied everything around her in excruciating detail, with a knack for seeing patterns and relationships in human relationships, and then taught the lessons that could be gleaned from them. Her most valuable legacy was her insight, and the evidence of it when she died was overwhelming. She willed some 370,000 documents—337 bankers' boxes and 64 file drawers' worth—to the Library of Congress.

Margaret Mead popularized her science—she was one of those rare individuals who could take an important but esoteric subject and make it into something interesting to the average person. She is remembered for her best-selling book *Coming of Age in Samoa* (1928) which was the result of her research into adolescent lovemaking among native tribespeople on the American-controlled Pacific island of Samoa. After its publication, her name became associated with sexual theory as she utilized her expertise to study American culture. Her talent was for putting sociological oddities or practices into the context of human history, such as examining whether there was an equivalent for toilet training in primitive cultures.

Mead was born December 6, 1901, in Philadelphia, where her father was an economics professor at the University of Pennsylvania. She had not yet settled upon a career when she arrived at Barnard College in New York, where she was inspired by an anthropology professor to traipse off into the bush and observe a group of natives before all the world's primitive cultures had been obliterated by progress. Her professor wanted her to study American Indians—easy and close to home—but she was fascinated by the South Pacific, and talked her father into coming up with the $1,000 (nearly $7,000 in 1990 dollars) required to finance her travel and research.

After her success with *Coming of Age* she became the preeminent anthropologist of her time and, from 1939 on, a prominent commentator on a whole host of social and political issues, from the Bomb to pre-marital sex. A popular public speaker, in some years she delivered as many as 110 speeches. She was often called upon to study practical questions, such as how Britons would accept a sudden influx of Americans when the U.S. entered the war against Germany. She wrote hundreds of magazine and newspaper articles and, for the last seventeen years of her life, authored a regular column in *Redbook* magazine.

The child to whom Mead gave birth on film was hard won. The professor started her life hoping to have six children, but had only miscarriages instead, and plenty of them. She was married three times. Her first husband was a theological student, her second was an anthropologist she had met in the line of duty, and her third was another anthropologist she met while she was married to her second husband. She eventually divorced the third one as well. When asked how she could put herself forth as an expert on the American family when she was such an obvious failure at marriage herself, she replied, "It's idiotic to assume that because a marriage ends, it's failed."

Some people found her cold and clinical, even shrewish at times. By contrast, she could also be extremely generous, and she managed to maintain many friendships, some of them from fourth grade, over all the years and miles of separations. She endorsed trial marriages for young people as long as there was an agreement of no children; and also supported decriminalization of marijuana, because she thought criminalizing substance abuse encouraged crime. Yet she also believed in a period of silent prayer in public schools, "in which each child could pray as his parents taught him to."

It was with her third husband, Gregory Bateson, that Mead produced her daughter and principal heir, Mary Catherine, in 1939, when she was close to forty. In addition to filming Catherine's birth, Mead insisted that the pediatrician of her choice be present, so he would begin his relationship with the child from the very beginning. It was an unusual request but the young pediatrician she chose agreed. His name was Benjamin Spock.

Mead approached motherhood much as she approached her work, making a practically academic study of raising Catherine, striving always to maintain a delicate balance between freedom and discipline. Mother and daughter enjoyed a warm, close relationship.

Margaret Mead died a grandmother, when cancer took her in November 1978 in New York, where she had been living for many years. Just five weeks earlier she had signed her last will. She was almost seventy-seven, and had worked a full schedule through 1977, when she opted to conserve her energy for her column and other writing. More than any other single force—any other social scientist, commentator, or philosopher—Margaret Mead helped the American family define itself in the mid-twentieth century.

She made a separate bequest to her daughter's husband, Barkev Kassarjian, of $10,000. It is not clear whether there was a schism in her daughter's marriage, or if there might have been some tax benefit or other goal. She left to the Library of Congress copies of all her publications and original manuscripts, as well as all her personal papers—miles of them, valued by the Library at about $96,000.

She left the rest of her estate, with a total value including her papers and books of $379,000 (or $644,300 in 1990 dollars), to her daughter Catherine, or in case Catherine died first, to her granddaughter, Sevanna Margaret Kassarjian. As executors she appointed her lawyer and a friend. But, she wrote, "while I have the fullest confidence in [their] business ability and judgment . . . I feel that they need guidance in connection with both my personal and professional writings and similar materials. I therefore request them to consult my friend, Dr. Rhoda Metraux, and my daughter . . . as to the publication, sale, or any other use of any copyrighted or uncopyrighted manuscripts."

Rhoda Metraux was more than just a friend. Mead had shared an apartment with her on Manhattan's Central Park West in her final years. They collaborated on the *Redbook* column, which offered advice, information, and common sense to millions of American women about family life.

Mead gave away quite a bit of money during her lifetime to establish grants and scholarships in anthropology. Within three years of her death she had assigned a $50,000 advance from her publisher to the Institute for Intercultural Studies. According to estate tax papers, she had also set up a trust for Rhoda Metraux, some thirteen years before she died.

Mead died owning an estimated $7,000 in personal property, and not much else that wasn't work-related and printed on paper. She had always lived modestly; an inventory of her furniture showed she owned quite a bit of broken antiques and modest art objects. Among these, a mahogany love seat, listed as very worn, carried no value. Her other furniture was eclectic, a smattering of early American, Chinese, Korean, African, and Eskimo. She died possessing a couple of hundred dollars' worth of silver service, and some costume jewelry. An 18-karat gold medal, the "Arches of Science Award" which she was given in 1970, was valued at $8,000, and was the most glittering bauble in her collection.

Mead was an optimist and often said she felt lucky to have lived during one of the most difficult and dangerous periods in human history. She believed that a certain amount of hardship, such as her many miscarriages, gave life its richness. These difficult times, she said, were like "just enough frost on the blackberries to make good fruit, but not enough to kill them."

Ethel Merman

ALTHOUGH SHE WAS NOT TO EVERYONE'S taste, more than any other performer in her time Ethel Merman embodied the soul and pure distillation of the raucous, spontaneous spirit of the Broadway musical in mid-twentieth century. Her unusual, clarion voice, likened once to a chorus of taxi horns, was huge, round, and self-assured, like her personality, and she could project even the clumsiest lyrics into every corner of every theater she ever played. As a gag she once stuffed her mouth with peanut brittle on the *Tonight* show and sang her usual clear, bombastic rendition of "There's No Business Like Show Business." The audience heard every word.

For all her brassiness, Merman, to her admirers, was considered a composer's and lyricist's dream, an enthusiastic belter who popularized and institutionalized some classic tunes of American theater, from "I've Got Rhythm" to "Everything's Coming Up Roses." She was self-taught, having learned to sing at home while her father played piano. She used to tell interviewers, "Hell, I just sing. I open my mouth and it happens. What more can I tell you?"

Unlike many artists who make it big, Merman never forgot her roots, or took on pretentious ways. She sidestepped fancy restaurants—"I'm strictly a meat-and-potatoes woman," she once said—was generous and nearly always picked up the check in restaurants, and continued to live with her parents in suburban Queens even after the big money started to come in. When she did move into a huge Manhattan apartment with an enormous terrace, she also moved her parents so they were living nearby, and she continued to shop at Lamston's, a five-and-dime where she liked to joke with the salesgirls at the lipstick counter.

Her will reflected this feeling for the old neighborhood and for her family, even toward those with whom she had fought from time to time. But don't get her wrong. Although she was religious, Ethel Merman was no choir girl. She was earthy, brash, and foul-mouthed—occasionally in a mean spirit when she was drunk. She was once seen on the streets of New York with her two children, yelling at them: "You don't wanna go to the zoo. You don't wanna ride the swings. What the fuck *do* you want to do?"

She was born Ethel Agnes Zimmerman in 1909—she added four years to her birth date after she became a professional singer—in Astoria, New York, a close-in working-class suburb of Manhattan and site of a movie studio that was only two blocks from the family home. Like her neighbors, young Ethel would walk down to the studio stage door, hoping to catch a glimpse of the stars, and dreaming of becoming one herself. Beginning her working life as a stenographer in a local auto-parts factory, she soon became personal secretary to the president. Years later, when she was established as a star performer, she liked to brag that she could still remember Pitman shorthand.

Without any lessons, she started her singing career in the 1920s as a cabaret singer and vaudeville performer. Her big break came in 1930 when she appeared in George and Ira Gershwin's Broadway show *Girl Crazy*. Audiences loved her style and enthusiasm, and the amazing things she could do with her voice. Singing "I Got Rhythm," she could hold a high "C" note for an entire sixteen-bar chorus, a feat that always brought the house down.

All told, she appeared in fourteen Broadway shows, most of them hits, and a few that wouldn't have been hits without her, sang thirty-eight songs, and appeared in some six thousand performances during her career. Although movies were never her medium, she did surface in a few, including the 1953 adaptation of her stage success *Call Me Madam,* and a role as the loud-mouthed mother-in-law of Milton Berle in the 1963 Cinerama comedy *It's a Mad, Mad, Mad, Mad World.*

By the time she died at the age of seventy-six, she had also appeared in four marriages, all flops, and produced two children. Things didn't exactly come up roses in her private life. In part this was because she was such a big star and enormous personality—the men she was attracted to could not accept a supporting role as Mr. Ethel Merman. Her first marriage, in 1940, to a Hollywood talent agent named William J. Smith, ended after only a few months. Her second, to Robert J. Levitt, a newspaper executive with Hearst, came closest to providing her with a perfect spouse, and he fathered her two children. Merman declared years later, "He was the only guy I really loved." But the marriage was flawed by Levitt's drinking and, finally, his dismissal by Hearst. The union was dissolved after nine years. Levitt remarried, had two more children, but later committed suicide.

Levitt and Merman's first child was Ethel, born in 1942. Robert Levitt, Jr., was born August 11, 1945. It appears that Ethel, the daughter, suffered most from Merman's fame, not an unusual set of circumstances. Young Ethel grew to resent her mother's success. Although she made a stab at an entertainment career for herself, it was half-hearted at best, and seemed to be based on some competitive urge. "I'll never amount to anything in show business, because my mother is a star. I don't have a chance," she once said. This sense of sadness prevailed in her life; in 1967 she committed suicide by mixing sleeping pills and booze. She was twenty-five.

Merman, in her typical response to life's tragedies, resented the unhappiness that her daughter had caused her, complaining, "How could she do that to me?" But Ethel Sr. did like Ethel Jr.'s ex-husband William Geary quite a bit (the couple had divorced shortly before the suicide), and remembered him in her will.

Husband number three was Robert Six, president of Continental Airlines, whom Merman married in 1953 and divorced in 1961 after she found out that he had "a broad in Honolulu." Merman also complained that he used to charge her and her children full price for plane tickets.

She retired from Broadway in 1961, telling friends, "I've had it. I've done fourteen goddam shows and what have I got to show for it? Three busted marriages and two kids I never had enough time for. When other dames were starting to enjoy an evening with their families, I had my dinner on a tray so I could get to the theater on time. From now on I'm living for Ethel."

Her last stab at romance was with actor Ernest Borgnine in 1964, and it lasted exactly thirty-four days. In her 1978 autobiography, she included a chapter titled "My Marriage to Ernest Borgnine." It was a single blank page. She would later encapsulate her complaint about all her marriages: "All men cheat."

If there was a man Ethel did love, it was her son Robert, although she disapproved of his "hippie" phase. She grew closer to him in 1972 when he married Barbara Colby, an actress whose career looked promising. But when the couple separated two years later, Merman blamed Robert. Then, when Colby was murdered in a random shooting incident in 1975, Ethel was disconsolate.

Merman died in 1984, after surgeons discovered an inoperable brain tumor that had been interfering with her speech. Her estate was valued at almost $1.5 million, mostly in stocks, bonds, and other cash instruments. Like a true New Yorker, she owned no houses or apartments, and her estate received a refund on her rent security of $2,050. She had lived most of her life in hotel rooms and apartments, from which she'd had the kitchens removed—because she almost never ate at home.

Her will ordered the auctioning of "all . . . tangible personal property . . . not otherwise bequeathed, including . . . jewels, jewelry, articles of personal adornment containing precious stones, furniture, furnishings, rugs, pictures, books, objects of art, and wearing apparel." The sale generated $120,000. This included three letters and a telegram from President Reagan that fetched $1,300; a framed letter from Dwight Eisenhower that went for $450; the prop rifle from *Annie Get Your Gun* that sold for $1,500; and some of her unbequeathed paintings and jewelry that were bought by friends eager to hang onto some memento of her life.

Signed four years before she died, her will lists bequests of $5,000 to "my friend" Josephine Treager, $2,000 to "my friend" Alice Welch O'Brien, and so on. O'Brien and Treager were friends from the days in Astoria. She left "my portrait of Panama Hattie [a role she played] by William Hicks to my friend Irving Katz"; "my gondola painting by Rubens Sandoro to my friend, Robert Lucas"; "my Bradshaw Crandall sketch of Bert Lahr and Ethel Merman in *DuBarry Was a Lady* to my friend, Thomas Hendee"; and her "Norwegian rose marble [mortuary] urns to my son-in-law, William Geary." In those urns rested the ashes of her parents and Ethel Jr.; Merman, according to friends, had had an argument with the cemetary where her loved ones rested so she took their ashes home, where they remained in her entry hall closet. Merman frequently "introduced" the departed family members to arriving guests. Those who might have been dismayed would be told by their hostess, "Where else am I supposed to keep them?"

All told, she left money or paintings of modest value to seven of her friends. She also left Geary $5,000. She left half of the rest of her estate in trust for her son, Robert, who was to receive the income and payments out of principal in case of emergencies.

The most touching part of the will is that Ethel Merman provided well for her daughter's children. Perhaps trying to make up in some way for the mother her daughter wouldn't be, she left the other half of the bulk of her estate to Michael and Barbara Geary. They were each to receive the income from a quarter of the estate, as well as the principal from Robert's trust unless he had children of his own.

Ethel Merman once summed up her philosophy about

music—and life—as "keep it short, sweet and funny." Her funeral expenses ran a thrifty $1,600. She was cremated, and a very small, private service was held at St. Bartholomew's Church in New York, where the only flowers were seventy-six roses, one for each year of her life.

Marilyn Monroe

NORMA JEAN BAKER'S MOTHER GLADYS Baker (née Monroe) had worked as a skilled negative cutter at RKO and Columbia Studios in Hollywood, where her history of mental disease and suicide in her family was of minor consequence. For most of Norma Jean's childhood—the pretty brunette was born June 1, 1926—Gladys was confined to mental institutions, leaving Norma Jean to ricochet among a succession of foster homes, where she was subject to neglect and even a rape attempt. Finally, at age nine, Norma Jean was placed in an orphanage.

At her death at the age of thirty-six, the former Norma Jean Baker, by now known to the world as Marilyn Monroe, still had a mother living in a mental institution. Even after her death, Marilyn was able to do for her mother what Gladys had never been able to do for Marilyn: provide support.

Decreed Monroe, "I direct my executors . . . to provide

$5,000.00 per annum [approximately $20,000 in 1990 dollars], in equal quarterly installments, for the maintenance and support of my mother, Gladys Baker, during her lifetime."

By any analysis, the financial care (part of a $100,000 trust established for Gladys by her daughter) was an act of affection, a commodity that lived in short supply in the sad existences of both Norma Jean Baker and Marilyn Monroe.

It was when she was sixteen and applying for a marriage license that Norma Jean received the rude shock that her mother had never been married to her father, whose identity as it was had never been properly established. He turned out to be an itinerant baker named Edward Mortenson, who was killed in a motorbike accident in 1929, when Norma Jean was three.

Seeking to escape her loveless adolescence as well as the dull confines of high school, Norma Jean eloped at age sixteen, with Jim Dougherty, a twenty-one-year-old aircraft plant worker. It, too, was a loveless relationship; the next year she attempted suicide. But in 1944, he went overseas as a merchant mariner, and Norma Jean took a job spraying paint in a defense plant. She also began to attract the attention of an Army photographer, one of several around southern California. The result, in turn, landed her in a modeling agency, where her hair was shortened and bleached blonde. Soon after, waiting for her divorce from Dougherty to become final, she plunged full throttle into a modeling career.

In August 1946, Twentieth Century-Fox signed her to a year's contract at $125 a week, and changed her name to Marilyn Monroe. She ended up with mentions in gossip columns, but few roles in pictures; even her bit parts ended up on the cutting room floor. Nor was her option picked up at the end of the year, but, ever eager, Monroe continued acting classes.

Columbia Pictures then took her on for a year. But that contract too failed to be renewed. To make ends meet, Marilyn posed nude for a calendar. Her fee: $50. The profit made by the calendar company: $750,000. The calendar had ended up selling one million copies.

But now Marilyn, or the calendar, successfully broke down the studio gates. Starting in 1950, she received a star build-up at Fox, where she had returned in order to play, typically, dumb blondes. Yet the roles grew larger; and so did her star profile. By 1952 she was famous enough to have her past exposed, and the press wasted no time in revealing that her mother was living in an insane asylum and that Fox's hottest new discovery had once posed nude for a calendar. The studio was nervous, but only for a moment. For the public didn't mind. The public loved Marilyn Monroe.

Yet—as too many corny screen star bios have remarked— even a movie Love Goddess can't take the public home with her. Monroe's next marriage, in 1954, was to Yankee baseball great Joe DiMaggio. By then, her fame had hit its peak, heightened by the image of her in *The Seven Year Itch* standing over the subway grating with her windblown skirt raised to her waist. Unhappily, the marriage was just as breezy as that air blast from the underground train—it was over in nine months.

The Seven Year Itch also marked the end of one phase of her career. In a demand for better roles she walked out of Fox and set up shop in New York, announcing the formation of Marilyn Monroe Productions. Farewell to roles as silly tarts, she insisted; she would now play Grushenka in *The Brothers Karamazov*. The press had a field day. Undertaking serious acting study with Lee and Paula Strasberg at their Actors Studio, Monroe also knew for the first time what it was to experience parental affection—from the Strasbergs.

Her education did not end there. She was seen keeping company with that most intellectual of New York playwrights of his time, Arthur Miller, author of *Death of a Salesman.* Once again observers howled, but it was Monroe who had the last laugh, albeit temporarily. She and Miller married in June 1956, by which time Fox had come back to her dangling a contract that provided much better terms. Now she could choose her own directors, so she selected Joshua Logan for the movie version of the stage hit *Bus Stop,* and, for the first time, scored a serious critical triumph. She followed with a flop, *The Prince and the Showgirl,* but the production did offer its prestige; the romance was shot in England and was directed by Laurence Olivier, who was also Monroe's co-star.

Next came what remains her best film, Billy Wilder's Prohibition comedy, *Some Like it Hot* (1959). She was back on top again, if only momentarily. After this success her career turned into a series of misfires—including one that proved disastrous.

Let's Make Love (1960) was better known for the back-stage romance of its principals—Monroe and matinee idol Yves Montand, husband of Simone Signoret—than for anything it had to offer onscreen. The 1961 drama *The Misfits* served merely as a curiosity item, a stultifying bore that happened to be written by Arthur Miller, whom Monroe would divorce shortly afterward. But then again, *The Misfits* also turned out to be the last picture to star both the King of Hollywood, Clark Gable, and its Queen, Marilyn Monroe.

During its production, delayed as it was several times owing to Monroe's emotionally distressed condition, she had to be rushed to the hospital following an overdose of sleeping pills, which she was mixing with alcohol. She consulted daily with a psychiatrist, except that this too offered only ephemeral relief. Shortly after the premiere of *The Misfits,* she entered the hospital for intensive psychiatric care. The press covered that just as luridly as it had covered the other misadventures in her life.

By the next summer, looking none the worse for wear, Marilyn Monroe was shooting another sex comedy for Fox, *Something's Got to Give.* The production stirred nothing but trouble. Monroe was habitually tardy—her reputation for being late, another symptom of her insecurity, was already well-developed in the early '50s. Frequently she would not show up at all. As a result, she was fired from the picture. Scarcely a month later, on the morning of August 5, 1962, her housekeeper opened her bedroom door and found Marilyn nude in bed, dead.

On the nightstand next to her sat a bottle of sedatives. The coroner called it an overdose of barbiturates and, in all likelihood, a suicide. And the press went to work again. In the ensuing years, it was widely—and snidely—reported that she was fatally attracted to the Kennedy brothers—John F. and Robert—and their exploitative treatment of her contributed further to her life's anguish.

It seemed, on every level, not to have been a happy existence. She was said to have wanted children desperately, but that was to be an unrealized desire. Her first pregnancy was tubal, and had to be aborted surgically. The second time she suffered a miscarriage. There have been reports that her Fallopian tubes were really tied after the first pregnancy, or else during an early muddled abortion. Like so many stories about Marilyn Monroe, this one has never been fully substantiated.

In the absence of a biological family, besides her *non compos mentis* mother, Monroe sought to remember the professional people in her life. She left her secretary May Reis

$40,000, and $2,500 a year to the widow of acting teacher Michael Chekhov (who had also trained Yul Brynner, among others). The bulk of her estate, 75 percent of it, she left to her acting coach, Lee Strasberg, with the remaining 25 percent to her psychoanalyst, Dr. Marianne Kris, "for the furtherance of the work of such psychiatric institution or group as she shall elect."

By the time her estate was appraised on April 16, 1963, Monroe was worth $92,781 (in the neighborhood of $370,000 in 1990 dollars), hardly suitable for someone who, despite her problems, had been the reigning star attraction of Hollywood for a decade. The household accessories of her leased Los Angeles residence at 12305-5th Helena Drive were valued at $2,486 and included some items of furniture that were quickly sold.

Not that Marilyn Monroe ever ceased to be a cash-flow commodity. In 1990, her image was still generating an estimated $1 million a year. So valuable is Marilyn Monroe in the current market that, in 1989, the two beneficiaries of her estate staged a bitter legal battle over who should serve as administrator, now that the original parties were gone. Lee Strasberg had died in 1982; and his second wife and widow, Anna, was accused of dragging her feet in approving contracts to profitably exploit Marilyn's image. There were documents waiting to be signed granting use of the *Seven Year Itch* image of the skirt swirling up around her on commemorative plates and dolls. Other licensing opportunities appeared to be lagging for want of decision.

At the same time, Dr. Marianne Kris had also died, and her stewardship of that quarter of Monroe's estate had passed down through a couple of hands to the Anna Freud Centre, an English institute that treats children and trains pediatric psychiatrists. The staff at the Freud Centre wanted no part of Anna Strasberg as administrator, because she was holding up possible income with her alleged delays so that, they claimed, their earnings had been cut in half.

Strasberg then filed countercharges arguing that any say to be had by Dr. Kris over who should handle her 25 percent of Monroe's estate died when Kris did, in 1980. In early 1990, a judge ruled that the Freud Centre should continue to receive income from Monroe's estate. Other issues in the dispute still remain unresolved.

Jim Morrison

ONE OF THE BADDEST—AND MOST CREATIVE
—boys of the rock-and-roll business in the late 1960s turned
out to be something of a concealed family man, as revealed by
his will. Jim Morrison had done just about everything possible
to outrage, alienate, and disgust the general public, and to
inflame the ardent fans of The Doors, the group of which he
was lead singer and chief composer. He spat at fans, exposed
himself onstage while he solicited sex partners, and pulled
stunts such as hanging off the balconies of hotels where the
group stayed while on tour.

But one day Morrison decided he had had enough and, in
1971, broke away temporarily from the insanity of the rock
world by moving to Paris, where he was intent upon working
on his first love, poetry. Except that iambic pentameter quickly
took a back seat to the seduction of living hard. After the

overdose fatalities of Jimi Hendrix and Janis Joplin, Morrison told people that he might be next.

So when news of his death in Paris ultimately surfaced, no one was terribly surprised. On the other hand, the mystery surrounding the cause of his death—he was said to have drowned in the tub—was never fully resolved. Yet, for the legal purposes of his estate, which proved to be substantial considering how durably popular The Doors' music turned out to be, he officially died in July 1971 at the age of twenty-seven. He is buried in Père Lachaise Cemetery in Paris.

His girl friend, Pamela Courson of Los Angeles, was his only heir. The will had been signed in mid-1968. In an affidavit filed a few months after he died, Courson revealed that they had been living together for six years: "I have considered that I was married to [Morrison] and that I was in fact his wife at the time of his death and am now his widow." She explained that they were going to get married, but felt that "the attendant publicity to a publicly registered marriage would have a detrimental effect upon the image [his managers] were trying to develop for him."

In other words, while Morrison acted the part of the angry, irresponsible, talented, and erotic young man his fans adored, he and Pamela Courson "decided that we would consummate a common-law marriage" under the laws of Colorado, which they did in Colorado Springs in September 1967. "We spent the night at a hotel, had sexual relations, and agreed that we would forever after be husband and wife."

Subsequent to that, she said, all her expenses were paid by Morrison, they lived together, and she ran up bills under the name of Mrs. James Morrison, or Pamela Morrison, even though the two were not officially married. When he died, she claimed to be "totally without money with which to live."

Morrison left Courson "every thing of value of which I may die possessed, including real property, personal property, and mixed properties." He was a 20 percent partner in The Doors, which was valued at $183,000 ($567,300 in 1990 dollars) at the time, but has since proven to be worth many times that. The will was just one page long and provided that if she did not survive him, or if she died within three months of his death, then the next person to inherit his estate would be his brother Andrew and his sister Anne.

Courson did outlive Morrison, by all of three years. She died in 1974 and the estate of Jim Morrison ended up passing to her family. Her father was named administrator of the estate, and brother Andrew and sister Anne went to see their lawyer. An agreement between the feuding surviving sides was said to have been reached, details of which were not to be revealed.

Zero Mostel

SOME OF ZERO MOSTEL'S MOST MEMORABLE roles had to do with money. In the 1964 Broadway musical *Fiddler on the Roof,* he portrayed his most famous character, Tevye the milkman, and sang the best-known tune from the show, "If I Were a Rich Man."

In the 1968 Mel Brooks satire *The Producers,* Mostel and co-star Gene Wilder concoct a scheme to produce what they deem will be the worst Broadway musical of all time so it will close on opening night, letting them pocket the unspent money raised from investors. In the first scene Mostel, a cup of coffee in his hand, looks out the filthy window of their disheveled office and makes out a figure moving on the sidewalk. He splashes a dollop of his drink on the window pane and rubs clean a spot with his jacket sleeve. The figure turns out to be a man dressed to the nines, about to enter a limo with a beautiful woman on his arm.

"That's right," Mostel screams at the man through the closed pane, his voice conveying cynicism and envy. "When ya got it, FLAUNT IT!"

Mostel, born in Brooklyn on February 28, 1915, as Sammy Joel Mostel, had it in spades, but never flaunted it. Instead he quietly socked it away, leaving an estate worth nearly $1.5 million to his wife Kate.

Mostel's first love was art. He painted and even taught art for a while, as well as working odd jobs—as a factory worker, longshoreman, tutor—to support his first wife Clara and the small studio he rented with two friends in Manhattan. His wife had the temperament, he later said, "of a spoiled daughter." She finally left him for good in 1941, after numerous arguments over money and the excessive time he was spending in the studio.

Mostel then moved back with his parents. While delivering art lectures at various New York museums and galleries, he discovered that he not only had a flair for insightful art interpretation but also for humor. He frequently left his audiences weak with laughter, and developed this gift into a way to earn three to five dollars at parties—money for paint and canvases.

In short order he was doing stand-up comedy at labor union functions, telling political jokes with a socialist bent. He was one of the first comics to use humor with a social slant. In 1941, at one of these appearances, he was discovered by a press agent, who got him booked that fall into one of the premier New York entertainment clubs, Café Society Downtown, at $40 a week. He was twenty-six years old. Drawing on the success of the Marx Brothers' zany names (Groucho, Harpo, et al.) and the fact that Mostel had no experience—he was starting from scratch—the press agent anointed him with the nickname "Zero."

A year later Mostel was the toast of the comedy circuit at a time, during World War II, when people yearned for laughter. He was earning nearly $5,000 a week from films, Broadway, radio, and club dates.

His second wife, Kathryn ("Kate"), was the daughter of Irish Catholic boardinghouse keepers in Philadelphia. She had also been an entertainer, kicking off her stage career at the age of eight in a variety act with four other little girls, playing movie houses around Philadelphia. At twelve she was dancing in a ballet troupe after her father died and the family needed money. The company was successful, and traveled around Europe. By age eighteen, she was working in Chicago where the ballet company was in residence.

When she met Zero at Café Society, she was a twenty-three-year-old Rockette dancer at Radio City Music Hall. She would later recall that Zero "was a man. All the other guys I went out with were boys, interested in sports, popular songs, me, or other boys. Never once had a political discussion crossed their lips. If Zero provided me with a feeling of security, it was mostly because he was so smart."

They decided to marry in mid-1944, but Zero was still hitched to Clara. Now that he was gaining notoriety, Clara wanted cash before she would grant him his legal freedom. But Mostel simply didn't have it. A friend, aspiring actor Karl Malden, offered to lend it to him. But, instead, Mostel agreed to give Clara a percentage of his earnings for the rest of his life. Lucky Clara.

Thus did the arrangement remain until the mid-1950s, when Clara required a chunk of cash. She was demanding $20,000, but Mostel took the matter to court, where he won a ruling that he need pay her only $5,268. Even that he had to borrow, because in the interim had come the Cold War and the witch hunt of Senator Joseph McCarthy and his House Un-American Activities Committee. Mostel was a liberal, although never a communist, but like many in the business he found himself out of work for several years. Their straits at some points were so severe that from time to time friends brought groceries to the family, which by now also included two boys, Josh and Tobias.

Although Kathryn and Zero were married for forty-one years, the relationship was usually turbulent. Burgess Meredith, who directed Mostel and was a longtime friend, said Zero adored Kate "with whom he fought most of his adult life. She was the closest and best part of him. And he of her, though their love was often boisterous."

Mostel had sexual liaisons with other women, but there is no evidence that he had any full-blown affairs that seriously threatened the marriage. He also had a huge, bellowing personality and traditional ideas about marriage: He didn't want Kate to work. He had insisted that she quit her career, and she complained that she was expected to wait for Zero in limbo while he lived his public life. She once said, "Every day of my life I have to fight like a tigress not to get pushed off the face of the earth by Zero." She apparently contemplated divorcing him more than once, but never took any direct action.

In his will, Kate was at last rewarded for her years of waiting. Mostel named as executor his lawyer, Sidney Elliot Cohn, who became his agent in 1963 when he was devising a television series that would feature himself, Kate, and their two sons, Josh and Tobias, playing themselves. Ironically, Cohn had been advising Zero that he had the potential to become one of America's foremost performers, but that he had "no future in the theater." So much for Cohn: Zero went on to make a fortune and a name for himself in two landmark Broadway shows, *A Funny Thing Happened on the Way to the Forum* and *Fiddler*. Mostel decided against the TV show on the first day of taping, dismissing the concept as insignificant fluff. He preferred more substantial roles.

The end came as he was about to open as Shylock, in an adaptation of Shakespeare's *Merchant of Venice*, perhaps the most dramatic role of his career. Mostel, always a big eater, in one of those life-imitates-art twists had put himself on a crash diet after the closing of a revival of *Fiddler*. In rehearsal for *Merchant*, he was adhering to a strict liquid protein diet (later shown to be unsound), eventually shedding eighty-nine pounds in four months. Members of the cast thought he'd begun to look haggard, and he seemed unusually subdued. Perhaps to help his diet along, he had been skipping meals and drinking gallon upon gallon of seltzer water.

The first preview performance at Philadelphia's Forrest Theater was on September 2, 1977. The next day while putting on his makeup for the matinee, he suddenly grew dizzy and nearly fainted. He wanted to go on with the show, but it was clear he would be unable, and was instead taken across the street to a hospital. After a battery of tests, the doctors decided he was probably suffering only from a viral infection.

Kate came down from New York the next day but Zero, already out of the hospital, persuaded her that he was fine and she returned home. He told her that he expected to return to the show in a day or two.

That night the symptoms returned. He was readmitted, but the staff doctors still could not diagnose what was wrong, except for exhaustion, and they suggested a couple of days of hospital rest. The night of September 8, one of the other actors in the show brought Mostel some art books, but the patient said he preferred lighter reading. The two were laughing about something when Zero suddenly complained of dizziness again, saying, "I better call a nurse." He reached for the bell but instead pitched forward, out of the bed, and onto the floor. He was rushed to surgery, where doctors attempted to install a pacemaker. They were too late. He'd suffered an aortic aneurysm (a blowout of the wall of the aorta) and died on the operating table. He was sixty-two. The doctors later speculated that his death might have been hastened by his starvation diet.

After taxes and other expenses, Mostel left half of his estate, $575,000, to Kate, with the other half to be held in trust and the income paid to her as long as she lived. When she died, the principal was to be split between Josh and Toby. Kate died nine years later, in 1986, of an asthma attack, aged sixty-seven. As his last wish, Mostel had told his wife that he did not want a funeral or memorial service. As he requested, he was cremated "like Einstein."

Audie Murphy

LIFE FOR HIM WAS HORRIFYINGLY SIMPLE during World War II. For the two years he served as a soldier, his sole concerns were killing and staying alive. He did both with a vengeance, and became the most decorated soldier of the war. Then the war ended and a different, much more complicated battle for survival began.

Audie Murphy was the quintessential American war hero. He was both a dedicated, well-trained killing machine and the freckle-faced American boy-next-door. He was the kind of soldier other soldiers admired for his courage and skill, but he was also childlike in his naiveté and self-effacement. In his will he asked that the only people allowed to attend his funeral be his wife and two children. The most celebrated, most decorated soldier of World War II said he wanted a "simple, plain and ordinary burial ceremony."

Murphy was born June 20, 1924, to dirt-poor cotton

sharecroppers in Texas. He was the seventh child—two more followed—in a family that lived far below the poverty level. His father wandered off one day and never returned, when Murphy was in his early teens. His exhausted mother died in 1941 when he was sixteen, and the family quickly scattered into marriages and orphanages. Murphy once said of his youth, "It was a full-time job just existing."

Unlike his siblings, Murphy seemed driven to be somebody. He displayed an interest in books and magazines and, although feisty at times and landing into fist fights, he was not a serious troublemaker. He was also a deadly shot with a rifle. When the Japanese attacked Pearl Harbor, he tried to join the Marines, but he was too short, only five feet 5 ½ inches, and at seventeen too young. He finally was inducted into the Army in 1942, and saw his first action in Sicily in 1943. In his best-selling memoir of his war experiences, *To Hell and Back,* Murphy wrote, "Ten seconds after the first shot was fired at me by an enemy soldier, combat was no longer glamorous. But it was important, because all of a sudden I wanted very much to stay alive."

He discovered that he had a certain coolness and calm fury in combat that made him fearless but calculated: He was able to throw himself into impossible circumstances and yet still survive. He once said, "When I get in a situation where it's tense and everything, things seem to slow down for me. It doesn't seem a blur. Things become very clarified." He had the sharp instincts of a hunter and flawless hand-eye coordination.

In all, he killed some 240 German and Italian soldiers during World War II. After Sicily he was part of the American force pinned down for months on the beaches at Anzio, Italy. Then his units moved due north, up the eastern border of France. He kept getting promoted, winning medals, proving himself repeatedly in battle. But when he wrote home, or when he was wounded and had to leave the front lines, he rarely mentioned his medals or exploits. He was the smallest, "cutest" hero that any of the military nurses had ever seen. He was shot once in the derrière and had to be hospitalized in Marseilles. A nurse who took a liking to him there remembered him as looking "like a child, anybody's kid brother." He was twenty years old but his size and smooth-cheeked complexion made him look a good five years younger.

There was a time when every schoolboy in America knew the circumstances surrounding the act for which Murphy won his greatest trophy, the Congressional Medal of Honor. He was a real-life Rambo. Referring to the actor Sylvester Stallone's movie role, Don Graham wrote in his 1989 biography, "Audie Murphy was the real thing, not some pumped-up aerobicized celluloid palooka."

On January 26, 1945, the small, under-equipped, underclothed unit that Lieutenant Murphy was commanding on a bitter-cold winter day suddenly found itself under attack by two hundred German soldiers and six tanks. Murphy ordered his men to retreat while he stayed on the front line directing American artillery by radiophone with pinpoint accuracy.

Only the Germans kept coming. The situation looked hopeless. The unit was going to be wiped out. Murphy had run out of bullets for his unit when he realized that a disabled armed vehicle, a tank destroyer, that was ablaze near him had a big machine gun on it, with plenty of ammunition. He climbed up on it and, while he continued directing the U.S. artillery barrage by radiophone, held off the enemy attack with the machine gun, at one point mowing down a dozen Germans. The attack dissolved, and Murphy was knocked off the destroyer by an exploding shell. He got up and walked away from the battlefield as the burning vehicle on which he'd been standing finally exploded in a ball of fire.

He came home from the war a much-decorated national hero. But although the real war ended in Europe in 1945, it continued to rage in his mind the rest of his life. He suffered from insomnia; in recurring nightmares he fought the war in his sleep. He hated his celebrity status and his subsequent Hollywood career, hated the insincerity of the people who were always trying to exploit him. Still, he was no longer so wide-eyed as not to see it was a way to make money and to find a steady parade of women to satisfy his sexual appetite, even during his marriage.

Murphy lived for a time in a guesthouse on the estate of the actor Jimmy Cagney, while he learned to act and launched a career in movie westerns. His book was published, and he married his first wife, an aspiring actress named Wanda Hendrix, in 1949. But the marriage didn't last and, in 1951, after a divorce, he married a stewardess named Pamela Archer. She was a Texan who for six years had pined for Murphy from afar, followed his career, and met him through a fluke connection with a friend. Marrying him was her dream come true. Although the marriage was rocky, she was Murphy's principal heir when he died.

They had two sons in the early 1950s, Terry and James. Murphy had appeared in several westerns for Universal when the studio decided to adapt his book for the screen. *To Hell and Back,* filmed in 1954 with Murphy playing himself, proved a great success commercially as well as critically. *The New York Times* reported, "The moviegoer glimpses, in the figure of this childlike man, the soul-chilling ghost of all the menlike children of those violent years, who hovered among battles like avenging cherubs, and knew all about death before they knew very much about life."

Murphy went on to make more than three dozen westerns, and took an unsuccessful stab at a television series in the early 1960s. Yet by then his life had begun a long arc of disintegration. His gambling habit, by some estimates, cost him $3 million during his lifetime. He was always hopeless with money, and the situation grew worse in the 1960s when he became mixed up with some mobsters. He was constantly facing lawsuits for unpaid bills and debts. For a while he was addicted to sleeping pills, grew increasingly paranoid, and saw himself involved in a screwy scheme to win a pardon from President Nixon for jailed labor leader Jimmy Hoffa. Murphy hoped to nab a payoff for arranging it. He grew so depressed at one point that he told a friend he was going to blow his brains out.

His last film, prophetically titled *A Time for Dying*, cast him, also prophetically, in a cameo role as the aging gun-slinger Jesse James. It was filmed in 1969, released in France in 1971, but not released in the United States until ten years later.

Two years after the film was produced, Murphy was on a business trip, flying in a private plane from Atlanta to Tennessee, when the end came. He was still making occasional celebrity appearances, and was attempting to put together a business deal that would pull him out of debt. He had devised a lot of crazy ideas, including a television series about a boy and a war dog, to star one of his sons. The pilot of the small aircraft, who previously had had his license suspended for running out of gas, drove the plane through a heavy overcast into the side of a ridge in Virginia. Murphy presumably never knew what hit him. He died May 28, 1971, at the age of forty-six.

His wife and sons later sued the pilot's estate and won a $3.2 million settlement—but there was no money to win, so the point was moot.

Murphy left his estate, which was presumably insolvent, to his wife Pamela except, strangely, for his personal belongings which he left to his sons, Terry and James: "To my sons . . . I bequeath all of my interest in any automobiles, horses, silver, chinaware, books, pictures, paintings, works of art, household furniture and furnishings, jewelry, clothing, and other personal effects."

His will contained a special provision disinheriting "each, any and all persons whomsoever claiming to be or who may lawfully be determined to be my heirs at law." This would have prevented any illegitimate children he might have fathered along the way from staking a claim.

The will also contained a provision that there be "no funeral service and only my sons in attendance at my burial at the graveside of my family plot at Forest Lawn Cemetery. If Pamela is then my wife, she shall also be present." He must have decided that this was a little cold and unfeeling so, eleven days after he signed the will, he added a codicil:

"I direct my Executor to take all steps necessary to arrange for a graveside burial with only my sons in attendance and Pamela also in attendance, if at the time of my decease she is then my wife. It is my express direction that no others shall be present at my burial, it being specifically intended to exclude any and all public officials and/or military personnel therefrom . . . I further limit my Executor in the amount of money [he] can spend for funeral expenses to an amount not in excess of medium priced funerals prevailing at the time of my death, to the end that the Executor will conform with my wishes to have a simple, plain and ordinary burial ceremony.

"By these directions, I do not mean to slight or be disrespectful to anyone, but, rather would prefer to have an unpretentious, unelaborate burial. It is my hope and expectation that during my lifetime I will have imparted to my sons such strength and character that they will desire the solitude of their own thoughts at my graveside at the time of my death, without interference from any other source."

The codicil was clearly written by Murphy. It sounds like him: simple, respectful, and heartfelt. It was almost as though he wanted his sons to have that experience he had had so many times, of burying a dead comrade on the field of battle, far away from marching bands and the rippling flags and the pompous speeches. In an interview two years before he died, Murphy revealed he was still obsessed with the war: "There, everyone understood the rules: You either killed or got killed. Here [in Hollywood], the rules are much more complicated. A person gets mixed up in contracts and talent and no talent and big egos and phonies and it is hard to live, let alone have a decent marriage and raise a decent family."

Audie Murphy did not get that simple burial. There was a memorial service in Los Angeles attended by more than six hundred people, including six other Medal of Honor winners. Then Murphy's body was flown to Arlington National Cemetery in Virginia, across the Potomac from Washington, D.C., where he was buried with full military honors and a large turnout of armchair generals and politicians in attendance, including the real thing in General Westmoreland and George Bush, then the U.S. Ambassador to the United Nations.

The only concession to his last wishes was the casket. There was no outer casing, which would have made it more expensive. Otherwise, Audie Murphy's heroism got exploited once more.

Louise Nevelson

IF EVER A WILL SERVED AS A FINAL ACT OF contrition for a life of bitterness, it was that of sculptress Louise Nevelson. By some accounts she had spent six decades agonizing over and mismanaging her relationship with her son and only child, and she seemed to try to make up for it in the end. Whether or not he deemed it to be worth the emotional abuse, the payoff was substantial.

Nevelson was a uniquely American creature, a completely eccentric, emotionally hag-ridden, ambitious, driven, foreign-born artist determined to enter the big time and stay there. She pulled it off, although not always with the smoothest of grace.

Nevelson was born Leah Berliawsky on September 23, 1899, to Russian Jewish parents in Pereyaslav, a small town near Kiev. The family, including an older brother and two younger sisters, emigrated to America in 1905, after her father had first spent three years in the new country working to earn enough money to bring them over.

She was five years old, and so depressed over her father's apparent abandonment of the family that she refused to speak for six months after he left for the U.S. It was the first of the many crippling depressions that would mark her life. Inexplicably, she would turn around and pull the same thing on her son.

Her father, from whom she inherited an ambitious, energetic nature, settled the family in Rockland, Maine, where he grew successful in the real estate business by buying up properties on credit. Louise was strikingly beautiful as a young woman, but maintained her virtue until she acquired her last name by marrying Charles Nevelson, brother of a New York shipbuilder who had come to Maine on business. It was for all intents and purposes an arranged union, one that Louise entered into with the clear intention of getting out of small-town Maine and into New York where she sensed her true destiny lay. Besides, he was rich: Nevelson worked in the shipbuilding business with his brothers, they were successful, and Louise would have servants to handle all the household chores.

For all the bohemian ways she would later adopt, Nevelson was a very demanding and ambitious young wife. Charles bought her an elegant one-carat diamond for their engagement, but she was offended that it wasn't bigger. Later, during the Depression, when the shipbuilding business had soured and there was less money, she refused to do her own housework, to pick up the slack.

Her son, Myron Irving Nevelson—or "Mike"—was born in 1922, after which Louise learned that she did not care to be so tied down. "I wasn't equipped" to be a mother, she later said. "I don't think I gave him any particular attention.

I don't think I understood what being a mother meant, as such."

This apparently showed. Mike grew up full of anger and resentment toward her, and she suffered a life of guilt and self-torment over her failure to be the supportive, nurturing influence that he desired.

Her art career commenced when Mike was young. She took voice lessons, initially appearing to be headed for a life on the stage. But her voice failed to be up to snuff, and she settled into studying art.

It was not long after taking her into their family that the Nevelsons decided Louise was crazy. She found objects in the trash, lumber, scraps of metal, and glued or nailed them together and painted them. She dressed in much the same way, as when she decorated a dress with a dickie made from a wedding napkin, or made a dress out of a burlap bag. This embarrassed her husband and even her son; when walking with her on the street, he took to strolling several paces behind her.

Not surprisingly, she also found marriage too restrictive. She was young and desirable, her husband was older, balding, and insanely jealous. They fought about sex and money.

Whatever else might have taken place between mother and son before September 1931, when the boy was nine years old, it was Louise's decision that month to go to Germany to study art, leaving him behind, that Mike would later remember as the low point. She deposited him with her family in Rockland without telling him where she was going. Then she called on the telephone from New York to announce it just before she sailed. He begged her not to go, but she was determined.

But it was in the depths of the Depression, when she and Mike lived together in New York after her estrangement from

Charles, that she really discovered the medium that eventually brought her so much success. They were poor, living in a raw artist space in Manhattan. Mike helped her scavenge through demolition sites looking for wood to burn in the fireplace and other discarded objects. "A piece of wire run over by a truck would be a jewel to her," Mike would remember later. She began to assemble pieces from all sorts of wood and metal trash, trying to express the feeling of the city through common objects.

Mike was shuttled back and forth between father and mother and other relatives, and suffered the predictable troubles: anti-social behavior in schools, running away a couple of times, being expelled. By the time he was a young man he had become an alcoholic. Mike loved his mother, but although she expressed unhappiness over having rejected him as much as she did, she also played the arrogant, self-assured artist, even with him. She once said to someone, within Mike's hearing, that no one had ever helped her in her career. This was certainly not true of Mike. The remark infuriated him and he complained to her on the spot. "I stand alone," she told him. "You are weak, and you need help from people, but I don't need help from people."

Nevelson fell in with a group of New York Depression-era artists who struggled to survive. Although she often expressed hostility toward men, she was not above using them for sex, money, and professional advantage, and frequently did so. Asked once during the Depression how she managed to continue dressing so well, she said, "Fucking, dear, fucking."

Her first big break came during America's first year in WWII, when she was forty-two and talked, or perhaps seduced, a major gallery owner into giving her a show. One of her first reviews was typical of the praise that would follow:

"Miss Nevelson injects, about equally, wit and a feeling of the primitive in her world which is stylized almost to the end of pure abstraction—but not quite."

In the 1950s she finally became aggressive about promoting herself, and it worked. She permitted her work to appear anywhere, even in beauty parlors; before long she was becoming noticed, and winning prizes. Still, she never quite got over the arrogant feeling that she had it coming all along, and had had to battle a world full of stupid, ignorant people to get the recognition and money she felt she had always deserved. At one of her openings in the late 1950s, when her pieces were selling for high prices, she complained, weeping, "It's too late, it's much too late."

By the late 1970s, however, she was the most popular public sculptor, and one critic observed that the country was in danger of becoming "one big Nevelson sculpting garden." By this time she had graduated into grand scale metal pieces. She had also been a guest at the White House, and won numerous awards including a National Medal of Arts from President Reagan.

She suffered from no lack of lovers during her life though she never married a second time. Even when she was seventy-six she was still trying to keep herself sexy—she had her breasts reduced to give her a more youthful appearance. Always exotic looking, she became even more so as she aged. She wore little makeup, often had her hair bound up in a bandanna, and took to wearing heavy, caterpillar-thick eyelashes. She also smoked thin little cigars and wore long robes, all of which gave her the appearance of an empress of art.

Nevelson could drink like a fish, and often did, but it was lung cancer that eventually killed her at the age of eighty-nine. Her will was simple, just a few pages of boiler plate leaving everything to Mike and his daughters. "Everything" was substantial, although little of it was in her personal estate. She had transferred most of her art works into a corporation organized by Mike that, when she died, reportedly owned $100 million worth of her sculpture. When her will was probated, it showed an estate worth $1.7 million, including three buildings that stood in New York's Little Italy, valued at $1.1 million, in which she had lived and worked for years.

Outsiders do not know if she ever asked Mike for forgiveness during her life, but it seems unlikely. She was irascible and unreformed right to the end, clinging to her bizarre way of dressing, her dark, brooding art, and her dark, brooding view of life. Discussing her grandchildren, she characterized her family life for the benefit of interviewer Jerry Tallmer in 1977: "I fulfilled my duties to nature, which I don't believe in anyway."

Dorothy Parker

DOROTHY PARKER MAY HAVE CONTRIBUTED
more to enliven the English language than any other American
writer since Mark Twain. She was the homegrown Oscar
Wilde, master of the witty remark, the throw-away line, and
the bon mot. Her humor was razor sharp even as a teenager,
and keen right up to the very end. Once, while suffering
through religious training at the Catholic school she attended
in New York, little Dorothy told the nuns that the Immaculate
Conception sounded to her like "spontaneous combustion."
Much later she had an abortion, complaining, "It serves me
right for putting all my eggs in one bastard." The epitaph she
chose for her tombstone was, surprisingly, a corny one—"If
you can read this you are too close"—the legend on many
automobile bumper stickers.

But for all her wisecracking, witty writing, and clever
repartee—it was the near-sighted Parker who once quipped,

"Men seldom make passes at girls who wear glasses"—her will was rather sober, matched only by the pathetic way she died.

Parker, born Dorothy Rothschild on August 22, 1894, during her mother's vacation in New Jersey, got her literary start writing photo captions for *Vanity Fair* magazine. There was a time in Parker's career, in the 1920s and 1930s, when quotes from her columns and magazine articles were on everyone's lips the way ad slogans sometimes are today.

She was a member and leader of an elite Manhattan group of writers, editors, and contributors to *Vanity Fair* and, later, *The New Yorker* magazine, who met nearly every day for lunch at the Algonquin Hotel to booze it up and challenge each other's wit. This group held center stage in the same New York literary scene of the 1920s and early 1930s that produced F. Scott Fitzgerald and a host of other contemporary novelists and social commentators.

Yet, with all the money she made, all the professional adulation she received, and the love interests that came her way, a friend was once moved to observe that Dorothy Parker was "a masochist whose passion for unhappiness knows no bounds." She apparently was a voracious lover of handsome men, and often became obsessed with her boy friends, sometimes driving them off and then sinking into fits of deep depression afterward. Her first marriage, to a Wall Street broker named Eddie Parker who drank a bottle of whiskey daily, ended in divorce in 1919 just as her audience and social circle were beginning to widen. "He was beautiful," she would later say of Eddie, "but not very smart."

Parker was so glib so much of the time that few people, if any, ever claimed to know who she really was. She had a wall of brilliant language to hide behind, and an arsenal of sometimes cruel and even malicious witticisms with which to torment her enemies. She was cute and stimulating to be around, but she was not especially well liked by those who knew her—a cross between Little Nell and Lady Macbeth, it was once said.

She seemed to suffer self-hatred on many levels, including guilt about her station in life. She was born to a well-to-do Jewish merchant and his gentile wife on New York's Upper West Side. She became a certified bleeding-heart liberal in the late 1930s, which is apparent from her will. She left it all to a civil rights charity, but it was no bonanza.

Parker earned large sums from her writing but was always pleading poverty. Nobody could figure out where she spent it, although it is entirely possible she frittered her money away on simple things like eating in restaurants most of the time. She lived in hotels much of her life, but was never given to ostentatious clothes, or cars, or other such luxuries. Her one big investment, a gentleman's farm in Bucks County, Pennsylvania, she ended up selling at a huge loss after pouring a fortune into renovating and decorating it.

Her best friend late in her life, playwright Lillian Hellman, said she had trouble "trying to figure out [Parker's] true-poverty-periods from the pretend-poverty-periods." Hellman said that Parker adhered to a view of the artist as, "the put-upon outsider, the . . . rebel who ate caviar from rare china with a Balzac shrug for when you paid." She left an estate that was more than a Balzac shrug, but not much more.

Several years before she died Parker had given Hellman a Picasso gouache and a Utrillo landscape, saying she was going to leave them to Hellman in her will, anyway. Near the end, in 1965, when Parker needed money, Hellman took it upon herself to sell the Picasso. It fetched $10,000, and she immediately took the check over to Parker. Two days later, Hellman got a phone call from a hospital where Parker had been admitted for some illness. The hospital officials said Parker claimed she could not pay the bill and they were calling to inquire if any of her friends might help. Hellman immediately went to visit Parker, who still insisted she was broke. Hellman reminded her about the $10,000 check. But Parker turned her head away and said simply, "I don't know."

"She *wanted* to be without money," Hellman said later. "She wanted to forget she had it."

Although she lived a long, full life (Parker was seventy-three when she died) it was purely an accident. She tried to kill herself at least three times after failed love affairs, only to be rescued always in the nick of time by the "lucky" appearance of a delivery boy or a friend. On the first try she slashed her wrists with a razor blade. It was her personality and style to ridicule and poke fun at everything so, after she recovered, she wrote:

> Razors pain you;
> Rivers are damp;
> Acids stain you;
> And drugs cause cramp.
> Guns aren't lawful;
> Nooses give;
> Gas smells awful;
> You might as well live.

But again she attempted suicide, a few years later, this time with sleeping pills. When she failed to show up for a lunch date the next day, friends went to her apartment and found her in bed, barely breathing. Her longtime cohort, the writer Robert Benchley, who'd been very sympathetic during the previous suicide attempt, this time told Parker, "Dottie, if you don't stop this sort of thing, you'll make yourself sick." After her third try, in 1929, it seems she gave up the suicide business, although that's anybody's guess.

In addition to death and love, Parker had a passion for small dogs. She owned during her lifetime a large collection of animals but always bestowed her greatest love on her canine friends, who were dachshunds, terriers, and a couple of mutts. It was one of these, a terrier named *C'est Tout*—appropriately enough, French for "That's All"—which was by her side when she died.

Parker tried to produce a legitimate heir but she miscarried once and never tried again. The father would have been the one man with whom she was able to have a lasting relationship—and he was bisexual. From time to time Parker hung out with a gay crowd, and it was during one of these spells that she met Alan Campbell, a young, handsome actor who was starstruck by Dorothy's wit and celebrity. They met and married in the early 1930s, thereafter working together on scripts and other writing projects. They broke up during World War II after Campbell was drafted. He was sent to London where he spent much of the war cavorting with the smart and literary sets and, Parker claimed, having an affair with a man he met there.

Although she filed for divorce in 1947, they maintained a friendship, and were reunited in the late 1950s to work in Hollywood on a film script. After this they decided to remarry, but Campbell had become an alcoholic and a pill abuser. The work for both of them dried up quickly in California—in part because of blacklisting—and Parker was no longer writing for magazines.

They both found themselves on the unemployment line

and came back to New York where Campbell died in 1963 at Dorothy's side, after a night of heavy drinking and pills. He was fifty-eight. They had known each other twenty-nine years.

Considering that Parker had once been the toast of New York, her own death was anti-climactic and painfully lonely. She also became a drunk in later years, and increasingly reclusive. She had settled into the Volney Hotel, an old tourist hostelry on Manhattan's East 74th Street, inhabited principally by widows and divorcees.

For a time she worked as a senior editor at Atheneum Publishers. But her eyesight had begun to fail, and the work didn't hold her interest anymore. She did her last writing in 1964, some captions for a magazine spread of paintings of New York, including one for a Manhattan sunset: "As only New Yorkers know, if you can get through the twilight, you'll live through the night." She signed her will a few months after that, in February 1965.

One night about two years later, June 6, 1967, she got drunk with an old friend, returned home to the Volney, and telephoned the friend to say goodnight once more in a slurred and sentimental speech. They found her the next morning in a pile on the floor, *C'est Tout* whimpering in a corner.

Parker died leaving an estate true to her nature. Apparently she spent most of what she earned, and left nothing in the way of mementoes to any of her friends or to family—if, indeed, she was in touch with any of its scattered members.

Parker owned sixty-five shares of *New Yorker* stock, worth $7,150. Beyond that she had almost $15,000 in cash in the bank, and $350 worth of uncashed royalty checks lying around the apartment—some of them seven years old—as well as that $10,000 check from Lillian Hellman, which she had never deposited. There remained some outstanding bills, too.

She owed the Volney $385, $24 to a drug store, $95 for newspaper delivery, and $65 to the IRS.

All told, she left an estate worth about $30,000 ($90,000 in 1990 dollars). After expenses, there was $20,000 remaining, which she directed to be given to Dr. Martin Luther King, Jr., the civil rights leader, although they had never met. (The money went to the NAACP; within a year King had been murdered.)

There was a funeral in Manhattan, and she was cremated in a yellow satin gown that, with a Balzac shrug, had been given to her by Gloria Vanderbilt, and which she had worn three months earlier at a sort of cheer-up party some friends had thrown for her.

Hellman delivered the eulogy, saying, "She was part of nothing and nobody except herself."

Cole Porter

THE MAN WHO WROTE, "LIKE THE TICK, tick, tick of the stately clock as it stands against the wall" knew from clock watching. Cole Porter was a stickler for detail and punctual to a fault. If someone was supposed to meet him at 11 o'clock and the date was five minutes late, Porter would probably be gone by then. His will was just as fussy, twenty-nine pages of specific instructions on how to dispose of everything, from clothing to a collection of scrapbooks.

Porter was born June 9, 1891, in Peru, Indiana. His mother was the daughter of a local millionaire who had large timber and mining holdings, and his father was a pharmacist who had little presence in his son's life. Two other children died in infancy. So Porter was raised an only child, doted on and coddled by his mother. When he began early to gravitate toward a music career, his grandfather complained, "I don't like all this music business. If the boy becomes a lawyer, I'll leave him my money. If he does not, he gets nothing."

Both Porter and his mother refused to give in to the old man's threats. She arranged for the boy to go off to a fancy Eastern prep school, and then to Yale. After that he made a stab at appeasing his grandfather by getting into Harvard Law School, but dropped out in 1915 to attend Harvard School of Music. He served in the French Foreign Legion during World War I, and started his music career soon after, cowriting his first musical with a college pal.

He wrote some 500 songs during his lifetime, many of them parts of Broadway musicals, including *Can-Can, Kiss Me Kate, Broadway Melody,* and *Silk Stockings.* He also wrote the scores for a number of films, including *Born to Dance, High Society,* and *You'll Never Get Rich.* His numerous dozens of love songs touched the hearts of millions: "I've Got You Under My Skin," "Let's Do It," "All of You," and "Night and Day," to name only a few.

Yet, for all the romance that flowed from his pen and his piano, Porter was a snob and a hedonist. His mother had raised him to think of himself as better than other children, to aspire to higher society, and he did. He married once, in 1919, to a beautiful, wealthy divorcee who was as devoted to having the high life as was Porter. They lived high on the hog in America and Europe, right through the Depression. But the good times they had were not necessarily with each other. Porter had scores of affairs with men, and frequented an exclusive male whorehouse in Harlem during the 1930s.

His life changed forever in 1937 when both his legs were crushed by a horse in a riding accident. Doctors wanted to amputate both, but Porter decided to tough it out. He suffered through some three dozen operations and excruciating pain during the next twenty years, trying to keep his body, and his dignity, intact.

Meanwhile, he continued to create, turning out some of his best work. His wife, with whom he lived part of the time, died in 1954, leaving him her estate worth about $2 million ($7.8 million in 1990 dollars). In 1958 his right leg finally had to be amputated; it sent him into a funk from which he apparently never quite recovered. He stopped writing and, for the most part, stopped socializing. He died in 1964 at the age of seventy-two.

Cole Porter was born with money, inherited some $9 million or so during his lifetime—from his grandfather (who did end up leaving him the money, despite Porter's career choice), and from his wife—and earned a second fortune from his writing. He did what he could to spend this big money by maintaining a lavish lifestyle, with posh apartments in Paris and New York, an estate in the Berkshires, and a home in California. Yet he still managed to leave a large estate, valued at at least $5.8 million ($20.3 million in 1990 dollars) for tax purposes, and probably worth much more than that, as time may tell.

For all the self-indulgence of his life, he turned out to be generous in the end, and rather modest. He wrote his own last "show," so to speak, insisting on a simple service and asking to be ignored in the town, New York, where he was most famous:

"I . . . direct my executors to arrange for no funeral or memorial service, but only for a private burial service to be conducted by the pastor of the First Baptist Church of Peru, in the presence of my relatives and dear friends. At such service I request said pastor to read the following quotation from the

Bible: 'I am the resurrection and the life; he that believeth in me, though he were dead, yet shall he live; and whosoever liveth and believeth in me shall never die.' [A]nd to follow such quotation with The Lord's Prayer.

"I request that the foregoing be substantially the entire burial service, and that neither said pastor nor anyone else deliver any memorial address whatsoever. I particularly direct that there be no service of any kind for me in New York City."

His will seemed to leave something to just about everyone, from friends to personal valets to cousins to universities and museums. He left $10,000 bequests to a number of people including Madeline Smith, his personal secretary of seventeen years, and to his chauffeur. He left $5,000 each to his valet and his masseur.

He left all of his clothing to the Salvation Army; records, books, books of clippings, and pianos located at his Berkshire Mountains estate were left to Williams College in Williamstown, Massachusetts; records, books, compilations of clippings, and pianos located in his California house were left to the University of California; the pianos in his New York apartment went to the Juilliard School of Music; books, original manuscripts, his recordings, and scrapbooks located in his New York apartment he left to Yale University; and to the Museum of Modern Art he left his collection of cigarette cases, many of them given to him by his wife, and some more of his scrapbooks. The museum refused these gifts and they went instead to the New York Public Library.

He left a number of personal items such as jewelry and silver service to specific people, including a diamond dress stud worth $400 to Douglas Fairbanks, Jr.

The rest of his personal things, furniture, jewelry, china, glassware, and the like went to his cousin, Jules Omar Cole, and Jules' son, James. He left the family estate in Indiana to James.

He set up a Musical and Literary Property Discretionary Trust that represented his copyrights and other interests in all those songs, shows, and movies he wrote or co-wrote. The beneficiaries of the income from this trust were eighteen different people, eleven of whom were under the age of fourteen when the trust was established. The will itself was signed in 1962, nearly two years before he died. The trust was valued at nearly $3 million.

There was also a trust that controlled the real estate he had inherited from his grandfather, which he left to his cousin and his cousin's son.

With all that disposed of, there turned out to be still more. When his executors went through his papers, they found 100 original Cole Porter songs—all of which had yet to be published.

Joseph Pulitzer

THE FUTURE PUBLISHING MAGNATE ARRIVED in this country from his native Budapest as a teenager ready to fight in the American Civil War. He had very poor vision, did not speak a word of English, and was so destitute that he slept on park benches in Madison Square in New York. He used to brag much later when he was a success that his wakeup call in the morning was the tap of a policeman's club.

Joseph Pulitzer fought in the Civil War on the Union side, and then, with a soldier from Austria, invested what little money he had in a train ticket that took him as far west as he could afford to travel. That turned out to be St. Louis, where he got his start in the newspaper business as a reporter for a German-language newspaper. By 1869 he was elected to the Missouri legislature, became part owner of the newspaper he worked for, and was on his way to earning his fortune in the news business.

When he died in 1911, at the age of sixty-four, he practically owned the world. He did own *The World,* one of New York's most prosperous dailies, and the St. Louis *Post-Dispatch.* He left an estate valued at close to $30 million, which would be equal to about $375 million in 1990.

New York was where Pulitzer coined a fortune that would allow him to live and travel like a king. But, unlike some of the robber barons with whom he could afford to rub shoulders, Pulitzer was no miser. He reportedly paid one of his editors a salary of $72,000 a year, equal to almost a million dollars in 1990. He left most of his fortune to his family, but they must have choked when they read the will. He gave away a huge percentage—hard to measure, but possibly as much as half—to employees and charities.

He bequeathed vast sums to some of his personal employees, including $25,000 (equal to $325,000 in 1990) to his "faithful valet," $50,000 ($750,000 in 1990) to his secretary, Alfred Butes, and $20,000 ($260,000) to Dr. George Hosmer, his "chief" secretary.

He also left $20,000 to the executors of his estate "with the request that they shall divide it as they see fit among those whom after consultation with the managers of the *World* newspaper, they shall select from among the oldest and the most faithful employees on that newspaper giving a special preference on account of loyalty and length of service and to employees receiving salaries of less than $100 a week. . . ."

He willed a similar sum to be similarly divided among the workers on the St. Louis *Post-Dispatch,* his other principal newspaper property. He also left stock in his publishing company to be distributed to the most deserving and loyal employees.

His will provided $5,000 to the Children's Aid Society

of New York; and other money for two major memorials: $25,000 "for the purpose of erecting a statue of Thomas Jefferson in the City of New York . . . the foremost democratic city of the New Republic"; and $50,000 for the erection of a fountain "preferably at or near the Plaza [hotel] entrance [to Central Park] . . . to be as far as practicable like those in the Place de la Concorde, Paris, France."

Five hundred thousand went to the Metropolitan Museum of Art, plus some stock in his publishing company, and another $500,000 went to the New York Philharmonic Orchestra.

He willed $250,000, the income from which was to help city youngsters in public schools to pay for college educations.

He also left a million dollars to establish a school for journalism in his name at Columbia University, an endowment that has endured to this day. Pulitzer scoffed at those who argued that good reporters and editors are born, not made.

Of all his bequests, perhaps the most enduring has been the Pulitzer Prizes which are administered by Columbia and awarded each year for excellence in many different fields of science, journalism, literature, art, and publishing. This part of the will went into some detail, offering prizes ranging from $500 to $1,500 (about $6,000 to $20,000 in 1990 dollars) for, for instance, "the best example of a reporter's work during the year, the test being strict accuracy, terseness, the accomplishment of some public good commanding public attention, and respect." Pulitzer saw himself as the conscience of good journalism, and once had signs posted in the newsrooms of his newspapers that read: "Accuracy, Terseness, Accuracy."

But, for all his concern about accuracy, his newspapers were breeding grounds for libel suits. When Pulitzer died, there were seventy-three such actions pending against the

World alone. Another eighteen were registered against the *Post-Dispatch.* In 1911, the year he died, the newspaper paid out $114,000 in libel settlements and awards, excluding legal fees and other costs.

Pulitzer was a moralist. Regarding his sizable bequests to outsiders, he left a message in his will for his family that may not have mollified them, but was touching and noble coming from a man who started with only a dream and a railroad ticket to St. Louis:

"During my life, and now by my will and codicils, I have given considerable sums of money to promote public or humanitarian causes which have had my deliberate and sympathetic interest. If any of my children think excessive such gifts of mine outside of my family, I ask them to remember not only the merit of the causes to which I have given and the corresponding usefulness of the gifts but also the dominating ideals of my life.

"They should never forget the dangers which unfortunately attend the inheritance of large fortunes even though the money came from the painstaking affection of a father. I beg them to remember that such danger lies not only in the obvious temptation to enervating luxury, but in the inducement which a fortune coming from another carries to the recipient to withdraw from the wholesome duty of vigorous, serious, useful work.

"In my opinion a life not largely dedicated to such work cannot be happy and honorable. And to such work it is my earnest hope—and will be to my death—that my children shall so far as their strength permits, be steadfastly devoted."

Ayn Rand

HOWEVER ONE FELT ABOUT THE 1980s—whether hating the greed, the ambition, and the conspicuous consumption, or relishing the financial action, the empire building, and the luxury—one of the people to thank or blame is Ayn Rand. Although she did not manage to live long enough to see it come to full flower, it was her philosophy of self-interest, imbedded in her novels romanticizing capitalism and condemning emotionalism, that inspired a lot of baby boomers to go out and grow rich. She was, for many college students of the late 1950s and 1960s, a cult figure of mythic proportion whose powerful novels left an indelible impression on their minds. Two decades later, in the 1980s, they hit their stride.

Rand was also a woman of mythic anger and bitterness. She managed to destroy most, if not all, of the important relationships in her life by constantly testing and challenging them. By the time she died, she had alienated just about everybody except one disciple, whom she ended up making her sole heir.

Her story, in light of the de-socialization of eastern Europe and Russia, is prophetic, to say the least. She was born Alice Rosenbaum to a merchant-class family in St. Petersburg, Russia, on February 2, 1905. Her father ran a chemist's shop. When she was old enough to harbor such thoughts, she suffered from boredom with her home, her family, her school, with St. Petersburg, with Russia.

She once said that her inspiration to write came in 1914 when, on a family trip to London, she found she could amuse her sisters by telling them imaginary stories about the lives of some show girls whose pictures she had seen on a poster. It occurred to her that she might be able to tell tales as a way of life and to spice up her dull existence. When she returned home she took up writing with a passion, conjuring up the people she wanted to know and become: daring protagonists, beautiful and smart, leading the life she thought most attractive—dramatic, full of adventure, and always with a happy ending for the heroes. She was driven, and believed she was destined for greatness.

As the Russian Revolution picked up steam near the end of World War I, she decided she was opposed to "the government or society or any authorities imposing anything on anyone." Freedom, she concluded in the context of the revolution, was the heart and soul of political philosophy, a way of thinking no doubt etched in stone the day armed soldiers burst into her father's chemist shop and stamped a red seal on the door, proclaiming it nationalized in the name of the people. She said she saw the look on her father's face, "one of helpless, murderous frustration and indignation—but he could do absolutely nothing . . . It was a horrible silent spectacle of brutality and injustice. I thought: *that's* the principle of communism. They were saying that the illiterate and poor had to be the rulers of the earth, because they were illiterate and poor."

The family savings melted away, and life became ragged, cold, and frightening. Food was scarce, clothing scarcer. By 1925 Rand had picked up a university degree, and had begun to study for a career in the film industry, when a letter arrived from a distant relative in the United States wondering what had happened to the family. She seized this thin chance to plot her escape to America. Granted a visa finally, in 1925, she made her way to relatives in Chicago.

When she arrived in the U.S. she changed her first name to Ayn, which was the name of a Finnish writer whose work she had read. Later, living in Chicago with her American relatives, she wanted to change her last name but keep her initials. She looked at her typewriter, a Remington-Rand, and decided to call herself Ayn Remington at first, but then switched it to Rand. She said she was certain she would be famous, and didn't want the authorities back home to take retribution against her Russian family for anything she might say or do in America. She never returned to Russia, and lost track of her family after World War II.

In 1926 she left Chicago for Los Angeles and, through a stroke of luck, met director Cecil B. DeMille, who cast her as an extra and, later, as a junior script writer. It was on the set of *King of Kings* that she met her husband Frank O'Connor, who was another extra and who would become her lifelong companion. He was also an artist.

The relationship was reportedly very sexual. She was clearly a dynamic, ambitious, independent thinker, and O'Connor was quiet and reserved. She thought about divorcing him from time to time, but she remained very dependent on the relationship, and was devastated when he died a few years before she did.

They had moved to New York in 1934 and the only time she left the city after that was when absolutely forced. She wrote a couple of plays and some film scripts, and read other people's plays for producers, before she started writing books. Her first novel to win recognition was *The Fountainhead* (1943), set in the field of architecture, which to her was "a defense of egoism in its real meaning." It had taken her years to write, and then was rejected by more than a dozen different publishers who found it uncommercial. When it was finally published most of the reviewers hated it. But *The New York Times* praised it, and gave it just enough of a push to keep it selling. Within two years it had gained such momentum that it stood solidly on the best-seller list. In all, the book has sold more than four million copies, and in 1948 was made into a film, starring Gary Cooper and Patricia Neal.

Her next book was *Atlas Shrugged,* a 1,200-page saga published in 1957. It further established her career as a free-market philosopher. Some reviewers loved her work, writing that it was epic and powerful and possessed the ability to change people's lives and ideas. It was even recommended as therapy for some psychiatric patients who were trying to cope with feelings of guilt.

But others condemned her "objectivist" view of the world as cold and unrealistic: "Miss Rand is all for survival of the fittest, dog-eat-dog . . . and other such bracing philosophies. . . . The destruction of the weak to the advantage of the strong is applauded." Gore Vidal wrote that her philosophy "is nearly perfect in its immorality."

She became a cult figure in the late 1950s and early 1960s when Ayn Rand clubs began to spring up around the country.

By 1965, courses on her books and ideas were being offered in eighty cities, and arrangements were under way to offer them to soldiers in Vietnam as a motivational tool. Admirers, some of whom would go on to positions in the federal government under Ronald Reagan, were dying for more and she began to publish a newsletter called *The Objectivist.*

One of those admirers who helped make her a household name was a younger man named Nathaniel Branden who, with his wife Barbara, became Rand's most devoted disciples from the time they were college students in 1950. She dedicated *Atlas Shrugged* to him. Branden eventually set up the nationwide courses, and ran the practical end of her efforts to expand her philosophies through his Nathaniel Branden Institute.

She and Branden also became lovers. Rand was, if nothing else, honest—she announced the fact that they were going to sleep together, even before they did, to both her husband and Branden's wife. She held so much sway over their lives that they accepted it, and lived with the arrangement for fourteen years, until Branden lost interest in Rand sexually—she was 61 and he was 36—and began a relationship with a younger woman. Rand found out about it in 1967. Having made Branden her principal heir—she had had no children by her own choice—she went crazy with jealousy and hurt. She cut him out of the will, and cut him and his wife out of her life entirely.

In 1972 she was reunited briefly in New York with one of her sisters who, still living in the Soviet Union, had run across her picture in a cultural exchange magazine. They hadn't seen each other for 47 years, but it turned out they had nothing in common and could not get along. The rest of her family had died.

Her husband succumbed in 1979, and she died three years later at the age of 77, after a bout with lung cancer and heart disease. At the funeral home she was laid out next to a six-foot-high dollar sign—her favorite symbol.

Like her philosophy, her will was short and rational, nothing sticky or emotional in it. It was a page and a half long, signed four months before she died. It left everything to Leonard Peikoff, a disciple she had met through a friend in 1951. Peikoff had become her closest associate and was in touch with her daily for the last four years of her life.

Her estate was valued at $877,000, including $188,000 she had inherited from her husband when he died, and about $130,000 value attached to her books, papers, and manuscripts. She had one book, *Philosophy: Who Needs It,* in the hopper and it was published posthumously. She had been working on a television mini-series based on *Atlas Shrugged,* but the project never got off the ground. She owned $9,000 worth of jewelry, including a gold brooch in the shape of a dollar sign worth $35 that she often wore, and a fur worth $4,500.

The only kin she had left was the surviving sister who still lived in Soviet Russia, in Leningrad. Executors of Rand's will tracked her down, basically to tell her that she had no basis to contest the will.

Babe Ruth

A CLOSE FRIEND ONCE SAID OF HIM, "I DON'T think he really loved anybody." But baseball player extraordinaire George Herman "Babe" Ruth made up for that shortcoming by liberally spreading around his copious affection. On the public side, he loved children and he spent many hours visiting those who were sick in hospitals or homebound to cheer them up. On the private side he was an insatiable womanizer and it got him into all kinds of trouble during his career, and he was hit with at least one paternity suit. His first wife, a waitress he had married when she was only sixteen and he was a twenty-year-old unknown, was constantly being embarrassed by press inquiries about his latest fling. Even the one legitimate child he fathered had a hint of scandal around her that was not finally resolved until more than thirty years after his death.

It is not entirely clear what Babe Ruth's estate may have been worth when he died. It had been a long time since he had played baseball when he succumbed to throat cancer in 1948, at the age of fifty-three. But, in a will that was signed just eight days before he died, he divided things up democratically among his second wife, his natural daughter, and a stepdaughter.

Ruth was born in Baltimore in 1895, but his fame, of course, came in New York with the Yankees. He set fifty-four major league records, two of which stood for more than thirty years. His first wife, Helen, could never handle his notoriety or his many affairs with other women. She had married a nobody, and ended up living with a personality bigger than the President. She suffered a series of nervous breakdowns, and eventually they drifted apart.

Before they did, Babe Ruth's first child, Dorothy, appeared, causing considerable confusion. The child literally showed up one day in the arms of Helen. The baby was clearly not a recent addition to the world—she was about two years old—and when reporters questioned Mrs. Ruth and then, separately, Babe, they received two conflicting versions of how old the little girl was. The papers went crazy with the story, and the Ruths offered little help. Helen insisted the baby was not adopted; but nobody had seen her pregnant and there had been no evidence of a child in her life until little Dorothy showed up in an advanced state of growth.

Not until she was nearly sixty years old, three decades after Babe Ruth died, did Dorothy herself learn the truth. In the meantime, back in New York, Helen Ruth had taken Dorothy and moved away from Babe. They were living with a doctor in Watertown, Massachusetts, two years after leaving Babe, when Helen was killed in a house fire. Dorothy, still a child, ended up in an orphanage in New York under the name Marie Harrington. Ruth soon found her and finished raising her with his new wife, Claire, whom he called Clara. Both

Helen and Babe took the truth of Dorothy's origins to their graves.

Fast forward to 1980: Dorothy is married and has a family of her own. She also has living with her an eighty-six-year-old woman—Juanita Jennings—who was part of Babe Ruth's retinue when Dorothy was a child. Juanita had married Babe Ruth's accountant, and came to live with Dorothy when her husband died. Two weeks before she died, in a truth-is-stranger-than-fiction twist, Juanita told Dorothy that *she* was her real mother. She had had an affair with Ruth when he was playing ball in California, and when she became pregnant, he moved her to New York and supported her.

Dorothy was Ruth's only child, as far as the record shows. His second wife, Claire, had a daughter named Julia whom he adopted and made one of his heirs along with Dorothy.

Ruth's last major league game was in 1935. After that he retired, reluctantly, but was never quite comfortable not playing or managing baseball. In 1947 doctors found a cancerous growth in his neck that was so far gone they could only remove part of it without killing him. He suffered through more than a year of treatments and pain. His final public appearance was in 1948 on the twenty-fifth anniversary of Yankee Stadium, the "House that Ruth Built." He died a few weeks later, attended by Claire, Dorothy, and Julia.

Ruth's will left "all my household furniture, automobiles, with the appurtances thereto, paintings, works of art, books, china, glassware, silverware, linens, household furnishings, and equipment of any kind, clothing, jewelry, articles of personal wear and adornment and personal effects excepting however, souvenirs, mementos, picture scrapbooks, manuscripts, letters, athletic equipment, and other personal property pertaining to baseball," to Claire.

He left the memorabilia of his career to his executors, two men who were friends and business associates, for them to "divide the same among such persons, corporations, and organizations . . . as they in their sole and uncontrolled discretions may deem proper and fitting."

He left $5,000 each (about $25,000 in 1990 dollars) to his wife and the two daughters; $10,000 to a sister, Mary Moberly of Baltimore; and $500 to his male nurse, Frank Delaney.

He set up a trust account for Claire and ordered that she receive an annual income from it of $6,000 as long as she lived. Anything over that was to be divided equally between Dorothy and Claire's daughter Julia.

The remainder of his estate went to Claire with the provision that when she died, ten percent of it was to go to the Babe Ruth Foundation to benefit underprivileged children, and the remaining ninety percent to be split between Dorothy and Julia.

The two daughters apparently did not get along, although they collaborated to the extent that together they sued some calendar- and baseball-card manufacturers for using their late father's name and picture without permission. They won their suit.

Jessica Savitch

FOR SOMEONE WHOSE LIFE WAS AS MESSY AS Jessica Savitch's when she died, she managed to leave a tidy little estate. The real bucks came *after* she died. Her death made millionaires out of her mother, her sister, and a handful of friends.

However Jessica Beth Savitch is remembered—she was the first woman to anchor an evening newscast—few people will forget the way she died. The blonde national newscaster for NBC, thirty-six, was on a date with Martin Fischbein, a thirty-four-year-old personnel executive at *The New York Post* whom she had met a few months earlier. They'd driven down from the city to New Hope in Bucks County, Pennsylvania, formerly an artists' refuge and now a cutesy tourist-infested river town dating back to the Revolutionary War.

They had dinner in a restaurant adjacent to an old barge canal that was usually dry, but this night had accumulated several feet of muddy water. It was Sunday night and the parking lot attendant was off duty. The weather had been tempestuous all day, rainy and windy, and it was still blowing rain in the darkness when the couple climbed into the car and Fischbein drove the wrong way out of the parking lot. Savitch's beloved dog and best friend, a black-and-white husky named Chewy, was in the vehicle with them. They drove a few hundred feet down a lane next to the canal when suddenly they ran out of road, and Fischbein's rented station wagon plunged off a twelve-foot-high wall, turned upside down, and landed on a log in the shallow water, sinking into the muck.

If they weren't knocked out by the blow of the roof collapsing on top of them, all three occupants would still have drowned because, among other things, the car had electric windows that were not designed to operate underwater.

An awful lot went wrong in Savitch's adult life. In spite of the tragic way she died, some people who knew her theorized that her death was almost a natural extension of what had been going on in the several years leading up to it.

Savitch was born February 1, 1947, near Philadelphia, although she lied about the date, shaving a year off her age because she had made a pledge to herself and a prediction to everyone else that she would make it big in the news business by the time she was thirty.

Hers was a prominent local family, in the context of a very small town at the far outskirts of the Philadelphia suburbs. On her paternal side were Jewish merchants who owned and operated department stores. Her father, who ran one such establishment in Newark, Delaware, died of a kidney ailment when she was twelve. Her mother was Italian, never felt part of the community, and moved Jessica and her two sisters,

Stephanie and Lori, to a small, middle-class community just south of Atlantic City, New Jersey, where she finished raising her family by becoming a nurse.

Savitch was driven and ambitious, both scholastically and professionally. Classmates found her "tightness" intimidating to be around—she was all work and little play. Later in her career, co-workers found her demanding and generally "impossible" to work with. She hit her stride in Philadelphia, her home city, and eventually found her way to network television with NBC in New York. She was the first on-air newswoman to break into the major leagues, with a combination of attractive good looks and a serious commitment to a career. She set the pace for television news operations across the country and, as her career grew, she found herself being cloned. At one point it appeared as though every station in the country employed a sexy woman wearing Jessica's streaming yellow hair and co-anchoring the evening news.

But she was an emotional disaster area, alternately vulnerable or egomaniacal. She even described herself once as "very emotional, insecure, unsure, overly sensitive to criticism, very high strung, nervous."

It isn't clear whether she was a heavy drinker, but Savitch developed a major cocaine habit by the late 1970s. She was married at the time to Mel Korn, a wealthy advertising executive who pursued a friendship with her after reading a profile of her in a magazine. Korn was divorced when he met Savitch, and helped package her and make her as popular as she ultimately became. It was he who guided her on how to dress and helped her sharpen her on-air delivery.

She finally married him in 1980. Ten months later he filed for divorce, complaining about her drug use and obsession with work. As she did with other scandals in her life, she told everyone a conflicting story about why the union ended, but never did her story have to do with drugs.

Soon after, she met Donald Payne, a successful gynecologist and obstetrician in Washington, D.C. She'd had a miscarriage and was seeing him as a patient for some minor surgery, before which she took out a million-dollar life insurance policy.

She told friends her sex life had never been better, although Payne had previously been ill with liver ailments and was rumored to be at least bisexual and possibly gay. To colleagues she never seemed happier, and was soon pregnant by Payne and desperate to have his child.

Both Savitch and Payne were reluctant to marry but did anyway. On her wedding day she confided to a friend, "I've made a terrible mistake." But she couldn't just walk out.

The marriage was rocky almost from the start. Then Savitch suffered another miscarriage. *Then* she discovered that Payne, who seemed distant and was a workaholic, was also a speed freak. In the process of discovering his stash of pills, Savitch let the fact of Payne's addiction out of the bag; and the ensuing professional scandal threatened to force the authorities to revoke his license to practice. Less than five months after they were married, she came home to discover his body hanging from a pipe in the laundry room, with Chewy's dog leash around his neck.

Her career was out of control, as well. A few weeks before she drowned, she showed up groggy for work. Because of her erratic behavior and messy private life, she had been reduced to delivering the live one-minute news updates that NBC broadcast twice a night during prime time. When the camera came on, her speech was slurred and she appeared completely unhinged. It was a major gaffe, since the news

updates were the best-watched news program on television—
and the most profitable—by virtue of being sandwiched between the highest-rated shows on NBC. Already in trouble,
Savitch this time was pressed to the edge.

Two weeks later, she told a close friend after a night of
reminiscing about the good and bad old days, "I feel like I am
dying. I just feel like dying." It sounded like a prediction. Two
days later, on October 23, 1983, the statement came true.

Savitch had irritated so many co-workers so many times
in her career that some of them felt no sympathy for her death.
One of them phoned another when he heard the first report on
the radio. "I have the worst news," he said. "Chewy's dead."

Savitch was immediately cremated, along with the dog,
and their ashes were later strewn in the Atlantic Ocean. The
funeral, which cost $1,816, was held with an empty casket two
days later in a small Jewish mortuary in a rundown section of
Atlantic City. Attendance was by invitation only and drew
twenty-five people, a scattering of friends and relatives. When
the service concluded, the funeral director had to chase the
mourning party out of the building. "Excuse me, folks," he
reportedly said. "There's another ceremony in ten minutes."

Two weeks later the Savitch family held a public service
in a church in New York. Four hundred people attended and
cost her estate $3,100.

Savitch signed her last will on December 11, 1981, four
months after her doctor-husband hanged himself and two years
before she died. She split her estate into thirds: one-third to her
mother Florence; one-third to her favorite sister Stephanie and
her two sons; and one-third to be split evenly among seven close
friends. They included: Mort Crim, a well-known national
newscaster whom she'd met in 1974 in Philadelphia when she
co-anchored her first national news program; Roberta Spring,

a newsroom staffer for NBC *Nightly News*; Dr. Patricia Payne Mahlstedt, the ex-wife of her dead husband, whom she'd befriended; Jean Sylvester, wife of a colleague of Dr. Payne's; Faith Thomas, a childhood friend; and Mary Manilla, who had been the first woman reporter at WCBS-TV in New York and a kind of role model and close friend to Savitch. Manilla had given up her news career to become a department-store merchandising executive, and remained one of the few people who tolerated Savitch's erratic behavior.

Jessica had a second sister, Lori, who also went into the news business, and with whom she had quarreled. Jessica told friends her sister was unappreciative of Jessica's help in Lori's messy divorce, and that Lori was unsympathetic when Jessica had her own problems. Lori was left out of the will.

Lori must be kicking herself yet. Savitch may have been erratic in her personality, but her finances were in great shape. She left an estate estimated at $1.7 million, including the million-dollar life insurance policy. She owned a condominium in Washington worth about $215,000, plus a house at the Jersey shore worth another $75,000. She gave the house mortgage-free to Stephanie. She had four and a half ounces of gold, two and a half ounces of platinum, an old sports car, $8,836 worth of clothing that went to Goodwill, $3,500 worth of furs, and about $27,000 invested in tax shelters. She also had some stocks and bonds and $355,000 worth of pension fund assets.

She owed $130,000 in back taxes, $196 in vet bills for her dog, $4,340 to American Express, and $110 to a beauty service. She was also in the middle of fighting an $85,000 back-tax claim by the IRS.

The real money, however, came several years later. In April 1984, her executors filed a wrongful death suit against eight entities, including Rupert Murdoch's News America

Publishing, Incorporated, owner of the *Post* and leasor of the car in which Savitch and Fischbein, a *Post* employee, were riding when they died.

Just before the case was scheduled to go before a jury, a settlement was reached to pay Savitch's estate a sum equal to what she would have earned in her expected lifetime. The *Post* had to pay more than $7 million. The restaurant, which had failed to warn its patrons of the dangers in its adjacent parking lot, had to pay $650,000; and the state, which failed to protect cars from falling into the canal, paid $250,000, the limit of its liability, for a total of $8.15 million.

Several of Savitch's beneficiaries, including the newscaster Mort Crim, said they planned to use some of this windfall to set up college scholarships in her name.

Savitch never had a chance to reach a calm and peaceful plateau in her lifetime, and may have had inklings of such. She once copied a quote from the biography of a famous advertising executive that apparently struck a chord within her, and was posted on her office wall: "Success itself is sort of a failure. You reach the end of the rainbow and there is no pot of gold. You get your castle in Spain and there is no plumbing."

John Steinbeck

JOHN STEINBECK LAVISHED A GREAT DEAL
of energy during his lifetime encouraging his two sons to reach
out and take hold of their lives, to be self-reliant, to seek
knowledge, and to experience all that life had to offer. Truth
to tell, he drove them a little crazy doing it. One summer he
was determined, he wrote to a friend, "to give them some
manness—by that I mean they are going to help me do things,
physical things, they are going to be let to wander if they want.
They are going to eat when they are hungry and sleep when
they are sleepy. As much as possible they are going to be
responsible for their own actions. They are going to associate
with men and animals and they are going to be treated with
respect—their ideas listened to and included." At the time he
wrote this, his sons were ages two and four.

Steinbeck tried to teach his sons a sense of responsibility,
but he clearly wasn't convinced the message was relayed. The

money left them in his will had strings attached: He wanted them to receive it when they were older and presumably more mature. From the grave, he was also going to teach them patience.

Steinbeck probably saw his sons, in the advance guard of the baby boom, as spoiled, especially by their father's success. Steinbeck was one of the most accomplished American authors of the mid-twentieth century, remembered best for his portraits of working class Americans struggling to survive during the Great Depression. His best-known work was *Grapes of Wrath,* published when he was thirty-seven years old, and seen as a document of social protest. It was the best-selling novel of 1939, the year it was published, won the Pulitzer Prize in 1940, and was made into a still-popular film starring Henry Fonda in one of his most indelible roles. The story of a farm family's forced migration from drought-eroded Oklahoma to California during the Depression, it has endured over the years and remains required reading in many college and high school English courses. In 1990 it was the basis of an award-winning Broadway production.

Steinbeck was born in 1902 and raised in California's "Salad Bowl," where several of his novels were set. He was inspired to write in college, and a bookstore owner in Chicago, who got hold of one of his early manuscripts and went into the publishing business in New York, helped put him on the map with *Tortilla Flat,* Steinbeck's first literary and commercial success. He also wrote *The Moon Is Down, The Wayward Bus, East of Eden, Sweet Thursday, Of Mice and Men,* and *The Winter of Our Discontent.*

Steinbeck had been nominated for the Nobel Prize for Literature during his heyday, but he did not win it until 1962, decades after his major work was published. He did not even know he'd been proposed and learned of his honor when he turned on television to watch the news. The joy he felt was tempered by the outcry against his selection that followed in the American press. *The New York Times* complained that the committee was out of touch with changes in the American literary scene. But the Swedes, and the rest of Europe, loved Steinbeck with just as much fervor as they had when his work was fresh.

Steinbeck worried that winning the prize could spell the end of his writing career—and it effectively did. Like Sinclair Lewis, Ernest Hemingway, and William Faulkner, all of whom had been unable to produce anything of real value after the prize was theirs, Steinbeck's career petered out.

He was married three times. His second wife, Gwyndolyn Conger, bore him the two sons, John Steinbeck IV and Thom, in 1944 and 1946. The marriage didn't last much longer after the second birth. The couple separated and eventually divorced. Steinbeck always hoped to win custody of the boys but never got it. They spent most of their youth with their mother, who was a heavy drinker and a potent force in poisoning them against their father. Steinbeck worried that living with their mother would make the boys too soft, too effete. The couple had fought over how the boys should be raised. He made efforts, mostly in fits and starts, to be close to them, and provide them a proper male role model, then complained that they weren't coming up right, that they were living lives of "sin and goldbricking." In 1961, when they were fifteen and seventeen, he decided to take them on a long trip around Europe. They took along a tutor, Terrence McNally, later a well-known playwright. "It will not be easy or soft nor by any means all pleasant," he told a friend. "But I think it is the best I can do for them. I don't think it will work magic but I do believe there will be some magic in it."

Whatever magic there was didn't last. Returning home, the boys decided to live with their mother again. And in 1964, she and the boys announced they were suing the author for an increase in child support. Steinbeck, his career in eclipse, his health deteriorating, his sons failing to reach the level of maturity he'd hoped for, became deeply depressed. Still, he stayed in touch with his sons and was supportive when John IV was busted on a marijuana charge in 1967.

Steinbeck married his third and last wife, Elaine Scott, whom he met in Hollywood in 1949. They were inseparable and she was with him when he died, suffering from emphysema and hardening of the arteries, in December 1968, at his and Elaine's apartment in New York City. Steinbeck, who once said that Elaine's "well-being and comfort and happiness are more important than my own," left her the bulk of his estate, including a house they shared in Sag Harbor on Long Island. In his last days he told Elaine, "You're going to laugh your head off when I'm dead. . . . Gwyn won't be getting any more alimony." It was Elaine, as literary executor, who approved the Broadway adaptation of *Grapes of Wrath*.

His son, Thom, and Elaine picked out the simplest wooden casket available, outraging the salesman, who complained: "You can't do this to Steinbeck!" He was cremated and his ashes dispersed in the wind at Point Lobos, California, near where he was raised.

Considering that his literary efforts had tapered off in the last decades of his life, he left a healthy estate: $1.4 million (about $4.35 million in 1990 dollars) as listed for estate tax purposes. His first bequest was to his sister Elizabeth, who lived in Pacific Grove, California: $25,000. Then he left the income from two trust accounts of $50,000 each to his sons. They were to be paid quarterly and then given the principal outright on December 31, 1974, when they would be twenty-eight and thirty years old, respectively.

He also left $5,000 to Ruth Fletcher who, the will states, was "now employed by me in my home."

The remainder he left to Elaine with the proviso that neither the house in Sag Harbor nor the New York apartment could be sold to satisfy the other bequests, "unless the same be absolutely essential."

Steinbeck loved writing, and when he talked about what he did for a living he could be at his most elegant and eloquent. His epitaph might easily have been lifted from something he once said about completing a project:

"To finish is sadness to a writer—a little death. He puts the last word down and it is done. But it isn't really done. The story goes on and leaves the writer behind, for no story is ever done."

Spencer Tracy

OF ALL THE FILM ROLES HE PLAYED IN A
total of seventy-three movies, the one that may best describe the
real Spencer Tracy was *Dr. Jekyll and Mr. Hyde*. A lifelong
alcoholic, Tracy is remembered for having been the sweet,
gentle, patient, almost priestly friend and professional co-
worker, as well as the raging, self-destructive drunk. On one
of his binges he locked himself in a Hollywood sound stage and
spent an hour destroying it, at a cost of about $100,000.

A devoted father and family man, yet he pursued a long
list of movie stars, including a teenaged Judy Garland, and
Ingrid Bergman, as well as whorehouse prostitutes. He considered his brother, Carroll, his closest friend. Still, more than
once he erupted into huge, violent fights with him, and once
tried to push Carroll out of a window. Tracy was nominated
nine times for Academy Awards for best actor and won twice,

yet he was wracked by insecurity and guilt, and suffered from insomnia.

Tracy was married and had two children. But in the last quarter century of his life one would hardly have known it. His first choice for female company was almost always Katharine Hepburn. It was said that they would have been married, and Hepburn would probably have been the main beneficiary of his will when he died at age sixty-seven in 1967. But when they first started seeing each other, in the early 1940s, Tracy refused to seek a divorce until his son, John, was grown and on his own. Besides, he was raised in a devout Irish Catholic home in Milwaukee, and divorce was not an option for him. Finally, when John was grown, it was Hepburn who didn't want to get married.

Tracy was born April 5, 1900, and got his start in theater in his home town, Milwaukee, putting on shows for the neighborhood kids in the basement of the family house, for a penny a ticket. He was thrown out of school often, usually for fighting, and talked about becoming a priest, a doctor, a lawyer, or an actor, even though he never set foot on a theatrical stage until 1921 when, as a student at Ripon College in Wisconsin, he was encouraged by a professor to try acting. Tracy seemed to have instinctive talents, and was also persuaded to join the college debating team. When the team went on tour and hit New York, Tracy successfully tried out for the prestigious American Academy of Dramatic Arts.

The founder of the Academy, who accepted Tracy after hearing him read, later said, "I took to the boy because he was manly and was capable of a strong dominating presence."

Tracy lived the life of the starving artist, impoverished that much more because he married early, in 1923. Louise Treadwell was also in the theater, a leading lady for a stock company that had provided Tracy with his first decent-paying job as an actor. The stock company folded soon after they met, but they convinced another group into hiring them both. They worked together much of the time until Louise bore their first child, John, nine months and two weeks after their wedding. They settled in Brooklyn.

When the boy was about ten months old, his parents discovered that John was completely deaf. According to Tracy's longtime friend, the actor Pat O'Brien, while Louise took the child to doctors to see if any remedy could be found, Tracy coped by going out and getting impossibly drunk. It was, according to his biographers, the first big drunk of his life.

He took a room in the staid St. George Hotel in downtown Brooklyn, stocked it with booze, and stayed intoxicated for at least an entire week. This would be his pattern over the years. He was a binger, and occasionally even well-organized about it. No matter the plan, often he had to be dragged home after he'd passed out in a bar or other public place. Once he'd recover, he would be fine until something else would tick him off, or make him feel guilty or insecure. Then he'd fly off the handle, busting up hotel rooms and landing in fist fights. Studio cops and executives frequently had to rescue him from potentially embarrassing episodes; a couple of times he had become so violent he had to be straitjacketed. At MGM in the '40s, there was even an ambulance and paramedic uniforms on hand, in case Tracy, or another star like him, had to be rescued before the authorities got hold of them.

Tracy's big break from stage into film came with talking pictures. John Ford discovered him in New York (playing beside Humphrey Bogart) in a play about prison. Ford was looking to cast a prison movie, *The Last Mile,* and although Tracy was, to his mind, "too ugly to be a leading man, and not ugly enough to be a villain," Ford gave him his first major role, of the six dozen or so that would follow.

The Tracys had a second child, Louise (they always called her Susie), in 1932. In the meantime John suffered more problems; he managed to survive a bout of polio. The family was comfortable, thanks to Tracy's screen success, so Louise had given up her acting career to devote herself fully to raising John and teaching him to read lips and, eventually, to speak. It became her life work: Using Tracy's money, she established and managed a philanthropic organization and clinic in the name of John Tracy, devoted to helping deaf people communicate.

It isn't clear how long Tracy was faithful to Louise after their wedding, but by 1933 he'd certainly been around, and around. His drinking and erratic behavior caused him to be fired from Fox Films. But it also got him to MGM, where he could get hold of better scripts and where he met Katharine Hepburn. Within two years Tracy had appeared in films that catapulted him to star status, *San Francisco* and *Fury*. He was now mobbed wherever he went, earning $5,000 a week, and his career was set. Not that he could relax about it. Louise once said he suffered from "fear of the future, a continual fear that any minute now they're going to 'catch on to him' and all this money is going to stop, that he's going to turn out to be just one of those flashes in the pan."

He was as uncertain about his family life as he was about his career. While he lived with Louise and the children on a ranch in Encino, and Louise accompanied him on some of his trips, in public Tracy would show up sometimes at restaurants and clubs with another woman, or in the case of Judy Garland, a fifteen-year-old girl.

Tracy met Katharine Hepburn in 1941, when MGM

found a script it thought would be perfect for them, *Woman of the Year*. The romance began soon after the shooting though it didn't become public until years later. The studio did its job of pumping out the line that the Tracys were still a happy family.

Over the years his son John not only overcame his deafness, but became an artist for Disney and a father himself, although he continued to suffer from periodic infections of one sort or another, and wound up living in a nursing home later in his life. Susie became a writer and photographer, eventually taking over her mother's benefactor role at the John Tracy Clinic. She had no children of her own, according to court filings.

The effects of the booze were beginning to overtake him, and Tracy's filmmaking began to slow down in the early 1950s. Hepburn, who told friends, "He may be a drunk, but he's *my* drunk," apparently got him to ease up on the alcohol; but the damage was already done. On top of that he had ulcers, part of his prostate had to be removed, and he suffered from kidney problems.

In the last eight years of his life he made only five films, including *Judgment at Nuremberg* in 1961. It was just after the end of filming this movie that Tracy signed his will.

He saw less of Louise as he grew older and spent most of his time with Hepburn, who read to him and for a period gave up her career to take care of him. It was clear he was dying, and he was a mess about it, according to Hepburn, who once told a friend, "He really, really is worried about dying. . . . [He] is really frantic about it."

Tracy made his last movie in 1967, *Guess Who's Coming to Dinner,* co-starring Hepburn, and directed by Stanley Kramer. It was a storybook swan song, making a big important movie with Kate promoting racial tolerance (they played liberal parents of a daughter who brings home a black doctor as her fiancé), and being nominated posthumously for an Oscar.

Tracy was so weak near the end of production that Kramer used a double, even in over-the-shoulder shots, to conserve the actor's energy.

According to official accounts, a housekeeper found Tracy at six o'clock the morning of June 10, 1967, dead of a heart attack, slumped over the kitchen table with a glass of milk beside him. But Hepburn would say years later that, "[Tracy's] engine stopped at three one morning. It just stopped—bang!"

According to the official record, Hepburn was the last one to come to the cottage where Tracy died, and in which she and Tracy had spent so much time together. She did not go to his funeral, even though she was devastated by his death. They had been each other's rock for twenty-five years.

Tracy's will, witnessed by director George Cukor, perpetuated the dichotomy between his public and private lives. Hepburn appears nowhere. The will sounds as if it was written by the contented husband of a contented wife with two happy children. He left his jewelry to his son and daughter, to be divided "as they may agree." In the original will he left to his brother, Carroll, "that automobile owned by me and used by me as my personal automobile, whichever automobile that shall be at the time of my death. I further bequeath to my said brother my wardrobe, or such part thereof as he selects."

Except two years later he signed a codicil that changed what he was leaving his brother to "all of the furniture, fixtures, paintings, and other articles of ornament and household use at 9191 St. Ives Drive, Los Angeles, and the two automobiles owned by me and used by me for my personal use, which are kept at said address. I further bequeath to my said brother my wardrobe, or such part thereof as he selects."

At some point before signing the codicil, Tracy had moved out of the family house and into a cottage on George Cukor's property, where he and Hepburn spent much of their time together. The codicil makes it clear that he had established himself outside the family home and owned property that was his, separate from that which was part of his marriage.

To his wife, he left almost everything else: "my interest in our residence or residences and such item or items as she may select from my remaining articles of personal, domestic or household use or ornament, including my remaining automobiles." He set up a trust which was to pay income to his wife as long as she lived. When she died, the children were to receive $25,000 each off the top, and then income from the balance of the principal. For some reason, Tracy did not want the kids to get all the money at once. He made them wait until they were forty-five years old before they could get more of the principal. In the case of his daughter she could have it all if she didn't have any children, or only 25 percent if she did have children. His son, John, would receive only 25 percent when he turned forty-five, whether or not he had children.

It isn't clear how much Tracy was worth when he died. But it must have been substantial because, when Tracy's wife died in 1983, court filings show there was still $300,000 held in the trust account. Each of the children received the designated $25,000 when their mother died and, since they were both over age forty-five, they also collected their shares of the trust principal. As it turned out, Tracy's daughter, Susie, never did have any children and got an additional $100,000. His son,

John, got another $50,000. At the time, John had another $25,000 in income due him, and Susie was owed another $31,000.

As part of the court filings in 1985, the trust account papers show that Tracy's movies were still pulling in money. His estate received more than $11,000 from United Artists Corporation for exhibitions of *Judgment at Nuremberg* and *Inherit the Wind.*

Finally, Tracy's will also had a provision that suggests he may have fathered children by some of his girl friends, or was concerned that he had. He specifically disinherited "all persons whomsoever claiming to be or who may lawfully be determined to be my heirs-at-law except such as are mentioned or provided for in this will."

Andy Warhol

ANDY WARHOL SPENT MOST OF HIS LIFE
making, chronicling, recycling, and selling the trash culture of
the post–World War II period—paintings of soup cans, multi-
colored photographs of celebrities, eight-hour films of a person
asleep, rooms full of helium-filled silver mylar pillows. But he
died surrounded by the classical treasures of the world. Estate
appraisers sent to his Manhattan townhouse to catalogue his
personal effects found room upon room of antiques, fine art,
jewelry, and collectibles. There were busts of Napoleon, Benjamin Franklin, and the Marquis de Lafayette; bronze statues
of animals, boxers, and dancers; a Chippendale sofa; a George
I wing armchair; an Aubusson carpet; American primitive
paintings; a woodcut by the Norwegian artist Edvard Munch;
mahogany furniture; marble-topped sideboards—the inventory
would have impressed William Randolph Hearst.

In the bedroom, in the folds of the canopy of a four-poster

bed, they found women's jewels. Drawers throughout the house were stuffed with watches, cigarette cases, and more precious baubles. The house was littered with shopping bags, cartons, crates, unopened and full of yet more . . . stuff. By the time they were finished, the appraisers had compiled a list of more than 10,000 items to be sold as part of Warhol's estate.

According to his longtime friend and executor of his estate, Frederick Hughes, Warhol "was a massive shopper. He considered shopping a part of his work, and every day he bought things that caught his eye on his rounds of flea markets and antiques stores, anything from nineteenth century sculpture and furniture to tiny little collectibles, like World's Fair items."

Antiques, Warhol once told a friend, made him feel rich. Whether he felt it or not, Warhol *was* rich—even beyond his wildest imagination. When the estate finally went on the auction block, ordinary objects fetched breath-taking premiums, simply because of the cachet of having belonged to Andy Warhol. His Rolls-Royce, which was appraised at $15,000, sold for $77,000. A collection of cookie jars that had cost Warhol perhaps $2,000 to collect, sold for a total of $247,830. A box of nineteenth century toilet-fixture catalogues sold for $1,500. A turquoise encrusted cow skull went for a staggering $3,600. The appraisers had estimated that the auction might bring in $15 million. Instead, it raised $25.3 million. The real estate Warhol owned when he died was estimated to be worth between $3 million and $4 million. And then there was his own art, of which he presumably had a sizable inventory, and which would have been worth many times what it was when he was still alive. As the writer Fran Lebowitz was given to observe, "Andy must be so furious that he is dead."

Warhol rarely referred to his upbringing—his pre–New

York days—confiding to a friend once that "I prefer to remain a mystery." He was born Andrew Warhola on August 6, 1928, in Pittsburgh, to Czechoslovakian immigrants with working class aspirations and slavish devotion to the Catholic Church.

Warhol grew up a mama's boy, and a bit on the sickly side. He showed an early aptitude for drawing; when he was home for periods of time because he was ill, or because other children at school had been tormenting him, his brothers bought him movie magazines that ignited a lifelong interest in Hollywood, New York, and mass culture. He started his art career at Carnegie Institute of Technology, first going professional as a young fashion illustrator drawing women's shoes.

After he landed in New York, Warhol burst on the scene as a revolutionary against Abstract Expressionism. He put forth as art paintings and sculptures of household products, such as cans of Campbell's soup and boxes of Brillo pads, dollar bills, and other commonplace artifacts. In the counterculture atmosphere of the 1960s his fame grew quickly, and he expanded his artmaking to film and books. Eventually he emerged from the rabble as a guru of the new underground culture, that embraced just about anything bizarre and kinky. He was still a fairly potent force a quarter century later when he died, in 1987.

Warhol lived among the fringe people. In the process he surrounded himself at the Factory—the name he gave his New York studio—with all kinds of artistic types and sycophants, some of them misfits and some psychopaths. But he was often accused of using people, feeding off the talent or celebrity of others and then discarding them from his life and business when he had wrung them dry. A few of these people got sore enough on occasion to storm into the Factory and threaten Warhol with bodily harm. A couple brought guns; there had been two incidents of rounds being fired off into the ceiling or a desk. One of these misfits, Valerie Solanas, woke up one day in 1968 to find herself frozen out of the inner sanctum, and concluded that Warhol exerted too much control over her life. She took a couple of pistols to the Factory in a brown paper bag, pumped three rounds into Warhol, and then put a hole in one of the other people working there. Warhol was clinically dead within an hour, but surgeons managed to save him, winning him another nineteen years of life, during which he made his fortune and became the high priest of the avant garde.

Warhol was gay, and claimed to have a romantic nature—he once said his heart had been broken several times. But he remembered none of his past lovers in his will. This may not have been out of spite so much as due to the sordid, cynical nature of his life. The fact also was that many of the people he'd been close to when he was younger had died of AIDS, including his last lover. Besides, Warhol was surrounded by people whose sex lives were casual and kinky, and his own sexual tastes were not much more conventional—he liked to watch other people in the act, and he had a special fetish for feet and shoes.

Warhol's career blossomed until about 1967. Then it hit a slump, and the art press began to get bored with him. *New York Times* art critic Robert Hughes complained about all the hype over his work: "If Warhol's superstars as he called them had possessed talent, discipline, or stamina, they would not have needed him. But then, he would not have needed them. They gave him his ghostly aura of power." Hughes's interpretation of the Warhol phenomenon was that he had assembled a group of lapsed and guilty Catholics into a parody of Catholicism in which "the rituals of dandyism could speed up to gibberish and show what they had become—a hunger for approval and forgiveness. These came in a familiar form, perhaps the only form American capitalism knows how to offer—publicity."

The man who rescued Warhol's faltering career and helped put him over the top again—and who would become his principal artistic heir—was Frederick Hughes, a self-taught art expert who had, like Warhol, shed his real background in the provinces; in his case, Houston. But unlike Warhol, Hughes reinvented himself as a patrician snob when he got to New York. Warhol met him in 1967; they took so well to one another that Warhol put Hughes to work running the Factory. Hughes offered Warhol a powerful and astute counterpoint to the dilettantist atmosphere there, and he was also soon drumming up some fat celebrity-portrait commissions for Warhol. It was Hughes who infused *Interview* magazine, which Warhol started only casually in 1969, with its character and, therefore, its success. When it was faltering and losing money in 1973, it was Hughes who suggested changing the magazine's format from an esoteric, artistic publication to one aimed at fashion-conscious, self-indulgent big spenders. *Interview* became the prototype of the rash of style magazines that hit newsstands in the 1980s. Warhol sold his share of the magazine in the late 1980s for $10 million. Hughes helped Warhol grow rich; he may even have saved Warhol's life: It was Hughes who thought to give Warhol mouth-to-mouth resuscitation after he was shot, while they waited for an ambulance to arrive.

Warhol died prematurely at age 58. It was partly because he procrastinated so long in having gallstones removed that his gall bladder became badly infected. He was apparently terrified of hospitals, and he refused proper care until he was in such agony that he could no longer function. He went into the hospital for emergency surgery under the name Bob Robert, so as not to alert the press. He died during the first days of recovery, apparently because he had been given an antibiotic to which he was allergic and his private duty nurse was not with him when he died. By the time she discovered he was in trouble it was too late.

If Hughes was personally broken up about Warhol's death he neglected to show it. With his lawyer he immediately went to Warhol's townhouse and got the will out of Andy's safe. When Warhol's brother, John Warhola, happened to call that day to speak to Andy, Hughes gave him the bad news, ordering him to stay away. "Don't bother coming to the house," John said Hughes told him. "We're putting a padlock on it."

But John and another brother, Paul, drove up from Pittsburgh anyway and, according to Paul, found Hughes and his lawyer "rooting through the place." Hughes told them they would have to stay in a hotel, and that they would meet the following morning.

At the meeting, the brothers learned that under the terms of the will Warhol had left a relatively measly $250,000 to Hughes, whom he named as executor, and also directed him to give $250,000 each to the Warhola brothers John and Paul. If one or the other had died before Warhol, the survivor would have gotten the other one's share as well.

The balance of Warhol's estate, the millions upon millions in houses, art, and just plain stuff, was left to "The Foundation for Visual Arts," which was set up in such a way that no inheritance taxes would have to be paid. The foundation was to be run by Hughes, with a board consisting of him, John Warhola, and Vincent Fremont, who occupied Hughes's former job as administrator of the Factory. The will, signed five years before Warhol died, specified that the foundation should be non-profit, that no private individual would be entitled to any of the profits, and that "no part of its activities shall consist of carrying on propaganda, or otherwise attempting, to influence legislation; it shall not participate in, or intervene in . . . any political campaign on behalf of any candidate for public office. . . ." It isn't clear whether this reflected Warhol's personal philosophy, or was instead legal boiler plate meant to satisfy the tax man.

According to Victor Bockris's 1989 biography of Warhol, Hughes told the brothers at the initial meeting that if they signed a waiver promising not to contest the will, they would each receive the $250,000. Paul, who believed his brother to be probably worth as much as $100 million, protested, but John was ready to sign. Neither of them had ever been to one of their brother's art exhibits. They apparently signed the waivers. When the brothers asked about a funeral, Hughes reportedly told them, "Oh, you can have the body."

Warhol once said, "Dying is the most embarrassing thing that can ever happen to you, because someone's got to take care of all your details . . . You'd like to help them, and most of all you'd like to do the whole thing yourself, but you're dead so you can't."

He got his wish to be buried next to his mother in Pittsburgh, bestowing, even in death, one of those fifteen-minute blocks of fame he believed everyone should have. The funeral home director boasted to a reporter that, "The competition is sure jealous today. It was all the talk of the funeral trade about how I landed the Warhol body."

Warhol was buried in sunglasses, a black suit, paisley tie, and one of his signature platinum wigs in a white-upholstered bronze casket, holding a small black prayer book and a red rose.

No one famous showed up for the small, family funeral in Pittsburgh. But Warhol was remembered fondly a few days later in a star-studded memorial service in New York's St. Patrick's Cathedral, the seat of the Catholic Church in the U.S., which would surely have seen Warhol burn in hell for the debauchery of his private life. A number of people, including Yoko Ono, spoke at the service. A minister disclosed that Warhol habitually spent Thanksgiving, Christmas, and Easter at a city church, serving food to the homeless. John Richardson, an art historian, told the crowd that Warhol "fooled the world into believing that his only obsessions were money, fame, and glamour, and that he was cool to the point of callousness."

Warhol had once written that he wanted his tombstone to be blank, or bear only the word "figment." Instead he got a small marble slab inscribed with his name and dates of birth and death. Someone tossed a copy of *Interview* and a bottle of Estée Lauder perfume into the grave before the casket was covered.

There's no way of putting an exact dollar figure on what riches Warhol may have bestowed upon Hughes while Andy was alive, but associate Bob Colacello in his 1990 Warhol biography, *Holy Terror*, states that Hughes worked for no salary, only expenses (as well as equity in *Interview* magazine, among other perks). Hughes's only outright cash inheritance was $250,000, although he stood to gain considerably from his role as administrator of the estate. Warhol also left no objects or money to any of the people who had been part of his life at one time or another. Two thousand people turned out for the memorial service in New York; his whole family showed up for the funeral in Pennsylvania, and except for John and Paul, not one of them were given so much as a print or an earring.

In fact, Hughes had to petition the probate court to be

allowed to buy the house on Lexington Avenue and 89th Street in New York that he had rented from Warhol since 1974 (Andy had lived there from 1960 until 1973), although as administrator of the estate, he must have been merely carrying out a formality—in effect, asking himself for permission. The value was set at $600,000.

Mae West

MAE WEST ONCE SAID SHE NEVER WANTED children "because you have to think about the child and I only had time for me. Just the way I didn't want no husband because he'd of interfered with my hobby and my career."

The '30s screen siren's hobby, of course, was sex. She liked to quip that "an orgasm a day keeps the doctor away," and, according to her biographers, she did in fact have sex just about every day. Her career was herself, a one-woman industry that made her famous and rich, and got her the men she craved.

But if Mae West's principal occupation in her life was herself—"My ego is breakin' records," she also once said—in death she showed how much she thought about others. Her will lists a number of cousins and other relatives, plus a few friends, to whom she left most of her estate.

She was born Mary Jane West in Brooklyn on August 17, you pick the year. She variously gave it as anywhere be-

tween 1887 and 1893. Her mother was Bavarian and her father, John Patrick West, was a professional boxer who later
owned a livery stable.

West was hopelessly stuck on herself almost from the
beginning, insisting on dressing up to go run an errand, watching herself eat in a mirror to make sure she was chewing like
a lady. She quit school in the third grade to enter vaudeville.
By the time she was twelve she was having sex on a regular
basis with just about anybody. She claimed she never got pregnant, or had venereal disease, because she always used a contra-
ceptive sponge of her own invention or insisted that her lovers
wear condoms.

By the time she was seventeen she was appearing on the
Broadway stage and earning a breath-taking $750 a week at one
point in 1911, equal to nearly $10,000 in 1990. She lifted
weights and appeared in acrobatic acts, as well as sang and
danced.

She married, but only once and she got over it rather
quickly. Frank Wallace was a vaudeville song-and-dance man
she worked with and wedded in 1911 on the circuit in Milwaukee. They'd been having a passionate romance during
which, however, she continued to see others. Soon after she and
Frank were married she took to sneaking off in the middle of
the night for purposes of infidelity.

But Wallace stayed hooked on Mae, and when they got
back to New York he agreed never to reveal the fact of their
marriage, and to let her continue to live at home with her
family—anything to hold on to her. Over the years they drifted
apart though, and eventually they lost track of each other until
the mid-1930s, when, at the height of her movie fame, their
marriage certificate accidentally found its way into the papers.
Mae denied knowing Wallace. But he pressed the issue and,

after a long, drawn-out legal battle, she finally admitted the marriage, settling up with him out of court.

She wrote and starred in her own plays in the 1920s, dealing with such forbidden topics as race relations and fornication. Her stage vehicles (she appeared in fifteen plays or revivals) aroused reviewers and community organizations to heights of outrage, and she even did jail time, although only eight days, on an obscenity rap for her play *Sex* in 1926.

In the 1930s she truly hit the big time, when she went to Hollywood and started making movies, a dozen in all. In 1934 she chose Cary Grant as her male lead in *I'm No Angel,* which earned her $340,000, and made his career. The following year she earned $480,000 (nearly $3 million in 1990 dollars), the second highest income in the country after William Randolph Hearst's $500,000.

She pushed for equality for black performers, and employed them liberally in her films and her personal life. She gave trumpeter Louis Armstrong his first big break in the film *Every Day's a Holiday,* often sharing meals with him in restaurants, which was scandalous in itself.

But she was, above all, a man-eater. As a woman in a powerful position—often controlling the script, casting, and production decisions on a film, running her shows with an iron fist—she playfully used the casting couch as a stud farm. In the 1950s she starred in a Las Vegas–style show that featured her surrounded by a cast of muscled-up body-builders. The show was built around the most risqué themes, and she chose the men who would work with her. The interview usually consisted of the job candidate stripping before he got the part. If she took a special interest in one, he soon found out he was obligated to service her every night, on command. Anyone who failed to keep up the pace got demoted or was out of the show.

"As long as they serve my purpose," Mae once said of men, "they're fine. But if they take up too much of my time, I eliminate them—see what I mean? I'm not going to stop being Mae West for any man."

But she did find a man who was able to thrive on her idiosyncratic lifestyle. He was a muscle-builder named Chester Ribonsky. She convinced him to change his name to Chuck Krauser for the show, and then to change it again later to a classier-sounding name—Paul Novak. He came to work for her in 1956, and his devotion to her, and his willingness to let her be herself, gradually won her heart. He became her body-guard, escort, lover, protector, cook, and, in the end, nurse. When she wanted to see other men, or wanted to be seen with other men to freshen the Mae West image, he would step aside. For twenty-seven years until her death, Novak worshipped and protected West.

She was a bit superstitious, sampling a number of different spiritual experiences, including fortune telling. When a psychic once told her that her nephew John and his mother had been asking how long Mae would live she got a little nervous, and spread a rumor that she had cut them out of her will. "That'll discourage 'em if they have any ideas of doin' away with me," she said.

Unlike Greta Garbo, Mae West kept throwing herself at her audiences long after she probably should have gone home and drawn the curtains. She made her last movie, *Sextette*, released finally in 1979. The critics demolished it. Typical of West, she said she hoped it would become an underground cult film like *Rocky Horror Picture Show*.

She died more than a year later, November 22, 1980, at the age of at least eighty-seven, after many years of coping with diabetes and suffering a couple of strokes. Paul Novak was with her when she died. At a service held in California, where she lived, a eulogist described her relationship with Novak as a "singularly tender love story," and recalled that West often said of Novak behind his back, "Paul's the greatest." Before she was buried Novak held her hand and complimented the makeup man; he said, "Miss West is pleased," and ordered an open casket.

Yet she left him only $10,000 in her will, which was signed fifteen years before she died. It wasn't that she didn't want to leave him more. According to a 1982 biography by George Eells and Stanley Musgrove, West had said she wanted to make Novak her principal heir, and she once told friends that she had a joint bank account with him, that eventually would hold half her assets. She even asked Novak to have a lawyer draw up a new will, making him sole heir, with the requirement that he take care of her ailing, alcoholic sister Beverly, whom West had been supporting for years.

Novak, however, apparently talked West into postponing the will change until Beverly's death. As a result, Novak had to assert his primacy in West's life in a palimony suit. He wound up with a settlement of $91,000—$41,000 in cash and $50,000 in stocks. But she undoubtedly bestowed benefits on him while she was alive. It's said they had a number of joint investments, and she may have transferred some of her estate to him before she died. She was noted for her generosity. She had a reputation for giving financial help to just about anyone who needed it. Even so, she managed to leave an estate valued at $1 million—$700,000 in personal property, $300,000 in real estate. She had an annual income of $50,000.

In her will she continued to spread her good fortune around, although who knows how the will would have read if she had rewritten it just before she died. To that nephew she had quipped might be trying to hasten her demise, she left $15,000; she left $10,000 to her personal secretary, who was a man, naturally; $25,000 to her alcoholic sister plus her automobile, all her personal jewelry, and her personal belongings; and $3,500 to the Mae West Fan Club of Ontario, Canada.

The rest of her estate she left in trust for her sister, the income to be paid out at the rate of at least $36,000 a year and "such additional sums, if any, as the Trustee [a bank] . . . deems proper or necessary for the health, support, and maintenance of my . . . sister, it being my desire that my sister be maintained in the same manner as I have done for her during her lifetime."

Then, when her sister died, half of what was to remain was to be divided into six equal parts and distributed among five cousins and her nephew. The other half was to be divided into seven equal parts and distributed to charities: the Motion Picture Relief Fund, City of Hope, United Crusade, Salvation Army, American Brotherhood of the Blind, Hollywood Comedy Club, and Cedars-Sinai Hospital in Los Angeles.

She was buried in the family crypt in Brooklyn, at Cypress Hills Cemetery where, in 1989, a news item reported that the mausoleum was falling apart and in disrepair. That would not have pleased Miss West, who once summed up her mystique this way: "It's not what I do but how I do it. It ain't what I say, but how I say it, and how I look when I do it and say it."

Tennessee Williams

THOMAS LANIER WILLIAMS WAS BORN MARCH 26, 1911, in Mississippi. His family always knew him as Tom. He changed his writing name to Tennessee as an adult because he thought his real name was better suited for a poet, not the playwright he had become, and he picked the name because his ancestors were closely linked to Tennessee politics and history. He left an estate worth $11 million.

Tennessee Williams was prolific. He got up most mornings and headed straight for the typewriter where he'd bang away for three or four hours. Most of his life he suffered from insomnia and his mornings would sometimes come in the middle of the night. He churned out in his lifetime an avalanche of material, including such impressive stage plays as *Cat on a Hot Tin Roof, Night of the Iguana, Streetcar Named Desire, The Glass Menagerie,* and *Sweet Bird of Youth.* He won two Pulitzer Prizes, the first for *Streetcar,* which, on any night of the week, is probably being produced in some language on some stage somewhere. Fourteen of his plays were adapted as movies.

The early years of his career were the better years for Williams. His tragic sense in his work was inspired by the pity and remorse he felt for his sister Rose, who suffered from schizophrenia and was given a lobotomy when she was twenty-four. Tennessee never forgave himself for allowing the damaging operation to happen.

So when Tennessee's behavior zoomed out of control from drug and alcohol abuse in 1970—he thought the actors he was watching on television were actually talking to him—and his brother Dakin had him institutionalized, Tennessee was furious. On the spot he cut Dakin out of his will—and announced it in a magazine article.

The two brothers could not have grown up more opposite, although they had been friendly as boys. Upon reaching adulthood however, Dakin, an Air Force lawyer with political aspirations, could not embrace his brother's lifestyle.

Williams had a few long affairs with men, but they failed to overcome the distractions of his success and his addictions. The one relationship in his life that he thought stable enough to outlast him and his work was with a woman, Maria Britneva, who later married into British aristocracy and became Lady Maria St. Just.

When they first met she was a young actress in London, daughter of a White Russian family that fled the Bolshevik revolution. They were introduced at a party in 1948 thrown by the actor John Gielgud. Lady St. Just remembered first seeing Williams, "crouched in the corner of the sofa and nobody talking to him. He was wearing one blue sock and one red sock, and he had these sad eyes. So I sat down. And he turned and looked at me and said, 'Who brought you up?' I answered, 'My grandmother.' And he said, 'My grandmother brought me up, too.' "

The friendship lasted thirty-five years, until his death in 1983, and the writings of the great American dramatic playwright were entrusted to the custody of a titled Russian-born Briton.

Williams signed his will in 1980, leaving to Lady St. Just the royalties from one of his later works, *Two Character Play*, and leaving her in charge, along with his attorney, of setting up a charitable trust to take in all his money and future royalty income and disperse it. Whether it was pretense or not, Williams was modest and directed that the fund bear not his name but the name of his grandfather, Walter E. Dakin, who had been an Episcopalian minister.

The fund was to be established "for the purposes of encouraging creative writing and creative writers in need of financial assistance to pursue their vocation [and] whose work is progressive, original and preferably of an experimental nature." Somewhere between the time he signed the will and two years later, not long before he died, Williams "disinherited" the University of the South at Sewanee, Tennessee, from having anything to do with the Dakin Fund. The head of the Creative Writing Department at the school would have played a hand in selecting the winners of the grants. But Williams apparently developed second thoughts and cut the school out of the will, leaving in charge the Creative Writing Chairman at Harvard University instead.

He was also alarmed about people tampering with his work. The will states, "It is my wish that no play which I shall have written shall, for the purpose of presenting it as a first-class attraction on the English-speaking stage, be changed in any manner, whether such change shall be by way of completing it, or adding to it, or deleting from it, or in any other way revising it, except for the customary type of stage directions. It is also my wish and will that no poem or literary work of mine be changed in any manner . . . except that any complete poem or other literary work of mine may be translated into a foreign language or dramatized for stage, screen or television. To the extent that I can legally do so, no party who shall acquire any rights in any play, poem or literary work of mine shall have the right to make or authorize the making of any changes in any play, poem or literary work of mine."

His sister Rose was still alive, living in an exclusive psychiatric home in upstate New York, when Williams choked to death on the cap to a bottle of sleeping pills in his room in New York at the Elysee Hotel. He was seventy-one, and she was seventy-three. The will specified that she was to continue to be cared for with no expense spared. "In addition to the payment of the normal expenses of maintenance . . . my Trustees shall pay to . . . [Rose] such amounts as they deem necessary or advisable for medical and dental expenses, clothing, and her usual customary pleasures as she now enjoys, including shopping trips to New York City, personal spending money, it being my intention that said Trustees shall provide liberally for her, not only for her needs but also for her comforts and pleasures."

After Rose, Williams also left a yearly stipend for one of his ex-companions, Robert Carroll, a Vietnam veteran who lived with Williams in the late 1970s. Carroll, a writer whose work Williams admired, was to get $7,500 a year for as long as he lived.

Dakin came last in the will. He was to get $25,000, but only after Rose had died and no longer needed caring for, a way of rubbing Dakin's nose in the family insanity that embarrassed him so. The will states: "I have intentionally made no other provision for my said brother as he is well provided for." Dakin contested the will, and settled for $100,000.

Dakin may not have gotten his brother's last dollar, but he had the last word in their lifelong tug of war. As next of kin Dakin had the right to decide what to do with the body. He ordered an open casket at the funeral, which Williams had specifically declined. And then, for the coup de grâce, Dakin buried his brother in the family plot in the hated St. Louis, where Williams had been locked up in the psychiatric ward. Williams had wanted to be cremated, with his ashes spread over the Gulf of Mexico, near the spot where his idol, the poet Hart Crane, suffering from writer's block, had killed himself by jumping overboard from a ship.

Index